MW01124972

Fun Thoughts
on Life

Learning That You are Enough
in a World of Too Much

Jennifer Anglin

Fun Thoughts on Life

ISBN 9781087285177
Printed in USA by Amazon.com

Dedication

I dedicate this book to Joan Smith. She saw this book in existence before I did. She persistently encouraged me to write this book. Her wisdom and guidance was the catalyst for my thoughts being in print. Thank you for seeing something in me that no one else did.

Preface

My real everyday life is funnier than anything I could fabricate in my own mind. I look at life with a glass half full attitude and laugh along the way. I love God, cherish my family, and love life. This book is a collection of true stories as I recall them. It is my hope that this book will remind you that miracles still happen. Believe that there is still good in the world. Restore your hope. Be refreshed that one person would put themselves out there to share their own stories of hope, faith, love, and disaster so that we could shed light on a dark world. Most of all, I hope that this book makes you laugh, makes you cry, and makes you think. Enjoy just a portion of my life as I know it.

Introduction

Welcome to Fun Thoughts on Life. These personal stories molded my authentic self. They led me to the realization that I am enough in a world of commercialization, hatred, judgement, rejection, standardization and expectation. It is my prayer that through reading my soul on these pages, you will realize that you are enough to override societal norms and be who you are. You can unapologetically be your flawed, awesome self. You can be #flawesome.

Prologue

I had the best childhood any girl could have ever hoped for. They did everything right in my opinion. I love them dearly and everything I am today is because of their grooming my wings and blowing wind under them until I was able to fly on my own. My daddy taught me that I could do anything I set my mind to and I believed him. My Momma taught me how to be a strong woman who is not jealous or judgmental. Because I had such a wonderful life and grew up knowing that I was adopted which meant that I was chosen and loved and wanted and special, I never had a need to know who my birth parents were. I had all I ever needed right in front of my face. My Momma and Daddy were enough for me.

It's a Girl!

I don't remember being a baby, but to hear my mother tell of the day she got me is one of the sweetest dialogues I have ever had with her. She and daddy had a lot of heartache trying to have children including miscarriages and one stillborn baby. After all that disappointment, I was a gift. I still like to lay under the Christmas tree each year to remind my family what a gift that I am. My parents got a call in June of 1970 that there was a baby available for them to adopt. In a scurried frenzy, my parents prepared for my arrival the very next day. I honestly cannot imagine the thrill that my existence brought to them. My mother commented about that day, "I walked into that office and sat down. They brought you in. I asked you if I could hold you and you held your arms out to me." It was love at first sight. I was hers.

When my momma and daddy were able to adopt me through a local children's home in Nashville, Madison Church of Christ, their lives were complete. They cherish me. I'd like to think that others cherish their children like my parents did for me, but I am not so sure they do. After so much tragedy trying to have children I was a treasure. I felt that so deeply growing up. I am still my parents world and I know it. My momma would rock me and tell me how special I was. She told me I was chosen, wanted, needed, and loved. She would tell me that I was adopted and that was exceptional because my birth mother was such a selfless woman. So that adoption was never a foreign word to me, my momma would bathe me and recount the story of my life. Adoption was always a part of who I am and what my family stood for.

Concerning my birth parents, I never wanted to search for them, or experienced curiosity about why I was given up or any other adverb that may have surrounded my early months. If I ever had the thought pop in my mind, I would just pray that God lay it on my birth mother's heart how grateful I am that she was so selfless to give me a life that was better than what she could provide at the time. Then I let it go.

I remember in college, a friend of mine was found by her birth mother. It did not end well.

I don't recall all the details of it but I do remember telling my parents that if anyone ever called the house asking about me, to tell them they don't know anything about me. I had all the family I needed or wanted and I had let God do the rest.

I was raised by the best. I firmly believe that contributed to my not having ill will toward my birth mother. The fact that I was rocked and told about my being adopted and special and chosen kept me from wondering. I never felt like anything was missing in my life or that I needed answers to fill in gaps in my personal timeline. I was full and needed nothing.

Another time in college, a friend I worked with said his mom gave up a baby for adoption the same year I was born. It would

13

have been a curious thing if I happened to be that baby. I figured out how to get my sealed adoption records and filled out the mounds of paperwork to release them. I made it all the way to the Office of Records in downtown Nashville, had the sealed brown envelope in my hands, and sat down at a table outside to open them. As I sat there and looked at that brown envelope, so official and plain, I thought about how wonderful my life had been, charmed and colorful-so different from that brown envelope. I thought about how fabulous my parents were and still are. I thought about how cherished I was and still am. I held that sealed envelope in my hands and prayed over it. I prayed that my birth mother, wherever she was, feel an overwhelming sense of peace and satisfaction about me and for God to let her know I was doing well. Then I took that sealed envelope

14

and handed it back to the secretary. I told her I no longer wanted the documents. I felt incredibly good about my decision and went along my way as happy as ever knowing God had handled it for me. I need not worry nor wonder.

Daddy's Girl

I have always been a Daddy's girl. I would match my daddy step for step no matter what he was doing. I helped him fix things, clean things, mow the yard, went to Ace Hardware with him, watched sports and the news with him; I did everything with him. Daddy never indicated that I was a problem. I am sure it took 3 times longer to complete a task with me under foot as it would have without me. Daddy was so proud of me. One of the favorite stories my parents like to tell of me is when I was three and we were at church. Daddy was a deacon and served the Lord's Supper every Sunday. One particular Sunday, I got away from momma and sidled next to

16

daddy, looked up at him and said, "I'll help you Daddy". There is no doubt in my mind that this moment was one of Daddy's proudest. I actually remember that happening. Maybe it wasn't that exact incident, but I certainly remember sitting in those church chairs, seeing Daddy serve our row and looking at him. He would always wink at me. He still has that look in his eye when he sees me. That look of sheer love.

Daddy also taught me how to pitch softball. He made a pitcher's mound and home plate that we used for years in the backyard. He taught me how to throw the ball so high that hardly anyone could hit it. He also taught me how to throw a slider, curveball, fast ball, and knuckleball in slow pitch softball. One coach asked my coach one year, "Did Jennifer throw that ball with no spin at all on it?" My coach, who went by Doc because he was a dentist, said, "Yes. Her daddy taught her how to do it." So from then on, the other coaches had their pitchers come and watch me pitch. I never did have a backup pitcher. I was it. We would play in tournaments and I could pitch all day long. Thinking back on it, it was really remarkable. Those pitches took me to be awarded the Most Valuable Player in the state of Tennessee in 1987. I got a big trophy and in that day, a trophy meant something. We didn't get trophies for participating back then.

Christmas

Christmas was always a big deal at my house. Of course I was an only child, and Santa was always good to me. I was told on Christmas Eve night how early I could wake momma and daddy up. I generally slept a couple of hours that night. The rest of the night I was up watching the rolodex type clock flip numbers over until it was time to wake up. Then, Momma had to put her robe on, brush her teeth, daddy had to go into the den and plug up the space heater so we wouldn't freeze to death opening presents. Then we would stand in the hallway, me, momma and daddy, and wait till Momma thought the heater had enough time to heat the room.

Momma gave the cue that we could go. It was always a great time. I got the best gifts. Always a doll and then other things, games, stuffed animals, toys, and clothes. One year I got a stereo and a Tom T Hall album. I listened to it over and over. My most favorite gift every year was a doll. I love dolls. I played with them until I was 15 years old. When I was 17, I got a gold coin ring. I thought I was the bee's knees with that. My parents always made sure I was happy. Love brings happiness and I was never short on love.

Grocery Store

Momma and Daddy owned a grocery store in White House with a longtime friend of theirs. Momma would go grocery shopping there each week and I would run straight to the back to look for daddy. He would carry me around or let me walk with him, once again matching him step for step the entire time Momma shopped. I don't know how many years we had the store, but I do know that daddy sold his part because he was working such long hours that he wanted to be home with me. I grew up being a priority.

Aunt Margaret

Aunt Margaret, my daddy's sister, lived next door to us. I loved her so dearly. She was my grandmother you could say. She worked at Genesco and we would go visit her at open house. We met her carpool buddies and other friends she had at work. We also got our cat, Muffin, from her coworker. That cat let me dress her up in all sorts of clothes and play with her like she was a human. Aunt Margaret always let me come over every Saturday and spend the afternoon with her. She let me make crafts, painted my fingernails, eat snacks, and talk. She was my first visitor after Momma and Daddy brought me home when I was 6 months old. She loved me as much as they did. I remember Aunt Margaret saying to me, "I never had children but I had you and you were all I needed."

Best Day of My Life

Today is the best day of my life. The reason is not because I am getting married, having a baby, leaving for vacation, or a major event. It is the best because I am alive and finding joy in sitting by the pool in the warm sunshine enjoying my family.

It's funny, people who spend time with me regularly will laugh when I say, "This is the best day of my life." I say it every day at some point. I may say it when I order my favorite ice cream or get a drink at Sonic. I may say it when I cross the finish line at a race, or while I sit on my deck and hear the birds chirping.

You see, if we wait till the big events in life to have a best day, then we spend most of our lives in mediocrity. It's all in your perspective. Look for the good in every day. Find joy in the little things. Happiness is a conscious decision we make every day. We can be like a sailboat tossed to and fro by our circumstances or we can decide to be happy and give thanks in all things.

May today be the best day of your life. I know it is the best day of mine.

Keep Your Eyes on the Prize

It is so important as we journey along life's pathway that we keep our eyes on the end goal. The end goal could be Heaven, marriage, successful children, getting through traffic tie ups, or reading a good book. Whatever the goal, it is important to keep it in our line of vision to keep us grounded and close to what we want to be and do in life. It helps us remain authentic and real. Sometimes we get so tied up in the forests of life, overwhelmed with the mass of trees, that we forget the one single tree that is the one we have been working toward. We lost our focus. A year's time is a very small dot on the scale of life when you look at the big picture. A year spent unemployed or battling for your life may seem like a huge thing at the time but on the scale of life, it is a small bleep of time.

Remember that. Keep your eyes on the prize so that when you get all wrapped up in what is going on right in front of your face, you will remember that this is a small thing. You will be able to pick yourself up and proceed on toward our goal of eternal life. Pain is temporary and so is happiness. Now joy, that is different. You can be joyful even in difficult times of your life. Learning to be joyful and not dependent upon happiness coming your way is a key to becoming your authentic self. Happiness comes and goes, but joy is forever.

Be Yourself

In high school, I remember admiring another student and trying to emulate them. As youngsters, we are especially impressionable and try hard to be like other people because we are trying to find our own way in life and figure out who we are. I would not want to go back to that time in my life. In fact, I was at the high school where my youngest daughter attends and an old friend stopped me in the halls and asked me about my tattoos. He said, "I never would have thought you would have tattoos." I said, "Well, that was when I was still trying to fit in." Old photos show my transition from fitting into societal norms into being unapologetically myself. I have noticed that my children, who were raised in a different generation, have become themselves much faster than I ever dreamed. I am glad that they did not spend time worrying about how they should look or act or be. They are simply themselves. In a world where you can be anything, be yourself, because everyone else is taken.

Do Your Best

I have lived my life hearing people say, "Do your best." That is an admirable motto to live by even when your best may not be good enough for everyone you meet. Your best is all that you have to give to the task at hand and that is enough. To those who feel like what you offer is not good enough, it is easy to become discouraged with life in general. The solution to this problem is in our internal mindset. We need to make up our minds that if we do our best, then we did well by our own standards. If someone has standards above what we can accomplish with our individual skillset, then the task needs to be given to someone whose skillset will exceed expectations. We should skip the guilt that we could not perform at a high enough level to achieve perfection on that person's scale in any given task. We were all created different. Some are good at mechanics and some are good at acting. We can't expect an actor to perform well at installing an engine in a car. Be who you are and let that be good enough. In a world of too much, be yourself and let that be good enough.

Live with Integrity

Integrity is doing the right thing even when no one else is looking. When you live with integrity, you live your life at a higher moral standard and make major steps toward cementing your authentic life. I personally cannot tell a lie even if I try. So much so that at work one day it was hilarious.

I had a particularly rough morning at the old folks home, and went in to the morning meeting with a scowl on my face. When asked what was wrong with me, I started going person by person explaining why no one helps me and what they are doing that they can't help me with my work. I basically threw everyone under the bus. Then, for decoration, I threw another coworker under the bus that wasn't even there. She was off that day. I felt really bad and started apologizing for being rude and brutally honest that morning. I explained that I had just had a rough day. Then, I called the girl that was not in attendance in the meeting and told her what I said about her, knowing that she would probably hear something hideous from another coworker that was far from the truth. We made peace with each other and we moved forward. I felt good about the situation because I knew that I had owned my mistakes.

Fast forward a week, and a different coworker called me into a private area and started telling me that a couple of others were murmuring about what I said in the morning meeting last week. I quickly shut that down saying, "Well they aren't talking about what I said because I called her and confessed what I said and immediately apologized for my lack of filter.

My coworker said, "Oh. You actually called and told her what you said?" Yes, I did because I live with integrity and it contributes to living authentically knowing that I am not perfect and neither is anyone else.

Own your poor behavior and move forward. People respect those who can admit wrongdoing. We are all a hot mess. Some of us just hide it better than others.

Bones

When things are going wrong for me, I always find it helpful to pray for God to throw me a bone. With dogs, a bone will keep them calm and quiet while they wait for the next thing to come along. Sometimes we, as humans, are just a notch above the animals. We need something to occupy us while we are waiting. God has always followed through with throwing me a bone when I ask for one. He may throw me a project that will occupy me for a bit, or He may throw me a bone in the form of a person to talk to that encourages me in the hallway before the next door opens. When you are discouraged, pray for God to throw you a bone and for the wisdom to identify it as a bone.

Spiritual Snacks

I love snacks. I consider a snack to be anything that is a little bite of something to keep me satisfied until my next meal. Our spiritual life is no different. We need snacks to tide us over until the next big time of study or chunk of scripture comes our way. Let's face it, life is busy and sometimes it is hard to carve out time to have a spiritual meal. But what we can do is snack on the word all day long. Leave your Bible open on your kitchen counter and every time you pass through the kitchen you look at just one scripture and meditate on it for a bit as you continue your day. Write a scripture over your light switch in your home so that you can get a quick bite of the word as you flip the switch. Get creative with spiritual snacks. Instead of beating ourselves up for not making time for spiritual meals, let's concentrate on meditating on snacks throughout the day.

Today in Kindergarten

I used to teach kindergarten. At the beginning of the school year, we were focusing on rules and procedures. After snack, I always had the children to pick up crumbs. It was twofold in purpose in that it cleaned the floor but also got out some energy for upcoming subjects. In my class, we referred to the procedure as "crumb catching". I noticed one young lad was sitting in his chair while the other children were picking up. I instructed him to pick up crumbs with his friends.

He replied, "I don't do crumbs."

I said, "We are in kindergarten now, we all do crumbs."

Blue Hair Bulletin

I used to be an activity director at an old folks home. We had a garden courtyard where flowers could be planted. I like to consider myself to be a hospice nurse for plants. I give them a peaceful transition to their death because I never remember to water them. If I do remember I over water them and they drown. I gave up on growing live pants a long time ago. One Blue Hair resident used to garden and they wanted to plant flowers in the courtyard. I explained my relationship with plants and she agreed that she would take care of them. I told her that she could plant whatever she wanted out there, that it was the Residents' garden. She replied that she wanted me to get the flowers but she didn't want Walmart flowers.

. She wanted to go to a nursery where the flowers were triple the price. I thought to myself, "Self, this will increase her quality of life, just take her to the nursery," $150 later we had a pallet of flowers that she told me she wanted to plant. I laid out all the supplies for her and instructed that she could take her time planting over the next couple weeks as she felt good. My husband and I ended up going up there on a Saturday to plant the flowers because I didn't want to sweat in my work clothes and she had not planted any of them. I then proceeded to instruct my Blue Hair Friend on how to water the flowers and turn the hose on and off. I explained to her that I was a hospice nurse for plants and if she wanted the plants to live she needed to water them. A week later, she came in my office and told me that the flowers were dying. I explained to her AGAIN that she needed to water them if she wanted them to live. I went back over the directions for turning on the hose pipe and I watered the flowers while I was out there. She and her friend watched me do it. She then told me that she wanted me to water the plants all the time. Per my boss's guidance, I told my Blue Hair Friend that we would just have to let them die. Appalled, she then stated vzthat she would, indeed, water them. Bless.

We Know What We Know

If we grow up in a family that is going to get ice cream at Baskin Robbins every Thursday night then we know how to live in a family that goes out for ice cream. We know what we know, which is ice cream with the fam. If we grow up in a family that does not go for ice cream, then the thought does not occur to us that other families go out for ice cream. We don't know what we don't know. When we go to school and have friends talking about going out for ice cream then we now know that people actually go out for ice cream with their families. Now that we know what we didn't know, we can do better. And by doing better we can invite our own family out for ice cream. I watered this down to ice cream but it can be applied to serious issues like domestic abuse. We don't know what we don't know about domestic abuse. But when we learn what we didn't know about domestic abuse, we can now do better. If we don't know then we can't do better about any given subject.

We don't know what we don't know. We know what we know. Until we learn what we didn't know, we can't do better. But when we learn what we didn't know, we are then empowered to do differently.

My Picture is on God's Refrigerator

Did you know that your picture is on God's refrigerator? In our society today, the refrigerator is a good place to know your importance to your family if you are a kid. Moms and Dads are pretty cool to put their kid's picture on the fridge. It is a front and center place to put a reminder of important people and important artwork and important notes about our favorite people, our children. Have you ever thought about the fact that God has your picture and my picture on His refrigerator? He does! We are His kids and we are important to Him. So naturally He has our pictures on His fridge. Let that sink in for a moment.

God loves us just the way we are. Society is the place where humans put unwarranted pressure on us to be or act or perform a certain way. God is not like that. Our worth is in Him. not in how we are here on this earth. Our worth is not dependent upon humans approving of us. This is a hard lesson for me. As a person who struggles with mental health, it is difficult for me to exclude what the world may think of me. It took me a long time to transform to my authentic self including tattoos that I had wanted for my entire adult life. I feared the judgement that comes from humans. I will never forget the first day I went to church after getting my arm tattooed.

The door greeter said to me, "Well, aren't you a hoodlum."

No, actually I am the same person that came in this building last week. It was hurtful what was said to me in a place that professes to be a hospital for sinners. The judgement at the front door was crushing to me. Since then, I have decided that God chose me to break the stereotypes of who is tattooed. I am the same fine, upstanding Christian lady that I was two years ago before I got the first tattoo. I was the same person after I finished my full sleeve on my arm. I am now my authentic self with my tattoos.

I want to attend the Outcast Church of Christ and sit with the sinners. I don't want to warm the pews. I want to be the hands and feet of Jesus and show others that I am not perfect and not a saint. Instead, I am the one who is willing. Here I am, Lord, send me. I am the one who has their picture on God's refrigerator and so are you.

Blowing Up the Kitchen TWICE

There is a really easy recipe for caramel pie. You simply put a can of sweetened condensed milk in a pan, cover the can with water and boil for three hours. Let me tell you from experience that you have to watch it and continue to add water as it boils. The milk becomes caramel in three hours. You can then open the can and spread it in a pie shell. VOILA! Caramel pie, or as my son at age 8 called it, Camel Pie. One time, I was making two caramel pies. I accidentally fell asleep on the couch while it was boiling. I awoke to an explosion in the kitchen and caramel was all over the ceiling, the floor, the cabinets, everywhere. I was completely dumbfounded. I knew I needed the pies so I started boiling two more cans and cleaning up the explosive caramel shrapnel all over the place. While I was cleaning, I forgot to add water AGAIN. So...I had a second explosion in the kitchen. Needless to say, I did not make caramel pie again for a long time. When I finally became brave enough to try again, I was careful to set a timer for thirty minutes to remind me to add water. This turned out to be a great method for me to have caramel pie without blowing up the kitchen. The funny thing is I had made this pie dozens of times before the double explosion and never had an issue.

Blue Hair Bulletin

When I drove the bus for the old folks home, one of the errands was to take them to Walgreens senior discount day. Upon arrival at work, the Blue Hairs would be piled up at the door asking when we were leaving for Walgreens. Taking senior citizens to discount day at the Walgreens is equivalent to taking children to Disney World for the first time.

Elder care is actually the same market as young children. Think of middle school lunch with a splash of toddler mentality. Let's discuss the dining room as an example. There is assigned seating and even when we are not in the dining room for a meal, folks still want to sit in their "scriptural seat". So if someone else is there for entertainment and another someone comes in and wants to sit in their dining seat, it can create pandemonium. Being a teacher by degree, I have been able to use my classroom management skills multiple times to diffuse a situation over someone "sitting in my seat." You see the dynamic here.

Blue Hair Bingo

Blue Hairs are serious about their Bingo. They think that if Bingo is scheduled at 2pm that it should start precisely on time lest the second coming of Christ is at hand and the activity director risks bodily injury via Jazzy hit and run.

If you can't keep up with the pace of Bingo calling, then you will be orally bashed by those who CAN keep up with the pace. You will be told that you are not good at Bingo and coached to repeat the verbiage, "I am not good at Bingo."

Blue Hairs believe there is no luck involved in bingo. You must pick "the right" cards that are winners for the day. If you don't win, then it is the Caller's fault.

We Know our Truth

Have you ever had someone question your version of a story? It is frustrating when we know we are telling our facts and people refuse to accept what we are saying. We know our truth. I have always heard it said that our perception is our reality and there are three sides to every story-my side, your side, and the truth. To be less abrasive, say, "I remember the incident differently than you do." You know your truth and so does the other party. Somewhere in between is what actually happened. It may reduce arguments along life's journey and help us become our authentic self when we realize that our truth is probably not as accurate as we believe it is, but realistically just our perception of the incident.

Gut-suckers

My panacea is the pool. I love the water which is odd because I drown when I was 10 and was brought back to life. I hang out at the pool daily during the summer months. I would even go after work. I see a lot of things at the pool. I see beautiful mommies playing in the water with their children. I see daddies throwing football with their boys in the pool. I see people relaxing and having a drink standing in the pool talking to friends. I will tell you what makes me sad at the pool-when I see gut-suckers. A gut-sucker is my own term for people that are very obviously sucking in their belly the entire time they are at the pool. What a miserable thing to have to do.

Very few people have a "pretty body". The majority of us are just normal people, with normal bodies. Surely by the time we are adults we can shake off the pressure of perfection and just quit sucking our belly in. I would hate to think that I have to hold my breath and contract my abdominal muscles for the entire time I was at the pool. Be you. Do you. Wear clothes that fit. Realize that we aren't looking at how you look in your swimsuit. We are noticing what a good mom you are playing with your children and creating memories. If you are sucking in your belly, then we are sad for you. Shake off the air of needing to have a perfect body. You have lived life in that body. It is precious. Relax. If someone judges you, that's their problem, not yours. Don't borrow trouble. Embrace your flawed, awesome self. Be Flawesome. You are enough, just the way you are. You are enough, in your swimsuit. You are enough at your finest. You are enough at your worst. You.Are.Enough. In a world of too much, you are enough.

Change

Change is hard. I have always been one who was invested in self improvement ,looking for ways to make a better version of myself. When things happen, I am always one to look inwardly at how I can make things better, not blaming others. I am also not into New Year's Resolutions. I feel like if I want to change something about myself, why not start now? I never have understood the mentality of "I will start that on Monday." God gives us a new day, a new hour, a new minute, a new second to make a fresh start if we are so inclined.

When you decide to change something about yourself, start small. If you try to change it all at one time, you become overwhelmed and tend to set yourself up for failure. When you tweak one tiny thing about yourself, you won't become overwhelmed or feel deprived during the transition. For example, I wanted to stop drinking so much diet coke. I drank a case a day so that was no easy task. I started by replacing one diet coke per day with one glass of water or some other liquid. Then I replaced two. For many years now, I drink only one diet coke per day and the rest of the day I drink water. I started small, setting myself up for success, and I made a life change by not overwhelming myself with too much.

Say No and Skip the Guilt

I have taught Bible class for a good number of years. Being a teacher by trade made teaching Bible class a no brainer for me. I rapidly began to dislike teaching Bible class. There was no discipline in the class like school nor was there a strong curriculum like in school. I continued to teach because I thought it was what I was supposed to do in the church. One fine day, I woke up and said, "No more." I quit teaching Bible class and skipped the guilt about it. It was not my thing. I took a few years off from serving directly in the church to give myself some time to think and explore what I actually like to do, rather than pursue the obvious womanly thing to do in church. I came to the conclusion that I like driving so I would get my commercial driver's license and start driving the church bus for youth trips, senior citizen trips and the like. I actually had a hard time getting my CDL for interesting reasons we will discuss later. Once I got my commercial license, I started driving all over creation in the name of the Lord. It was my thing. I loved doing it. I loved driving our youth group to retreats, camps, and events. I also loved driving our church members to pack boxes for disaster relief.

From that day forward, when asked to teach Bible class, I would say, "God is using me in other areas right now." I would then proceed to skip the guilt. Read that again-God is using me in other areas right now. Then skip the guilt. That is strong commentary when asked to give of your time. This does not just apply to church work. For example, if the room mother asks you to make cupcakes for the class party and you despise baking, then simply say, "I am better at buying plates and napkins." If that is already taken, say, "I will help next time." THEN...SKIP the guilt.

Why do People Lie

Have you ever been talking to someone and knew they were lying? I think we all have been in that situation and even lied ourselves, but compulsive liars are especially tricky. Personally, I can't lie even if it incriminates me. My inability to lie has moved me closer to my authentic self. It makes me "real" to others when I openly admit that I made a mistake or said the wrong thing.

I am suggesting that people lie because they don't think the truth will be good enough. Read that again. Meditate on it. Your child tells you that they didn't write on the walls with sharpie because they are afraid you would be disappointed in them. The truth isn't good enough. Using a child as an example may not be the best, so let's throw one out for adults: Someone invites you to go to a concert. You simply don't want to go. You have a lot going on for a couple of weeks before the concert and you don't want to overbook yourself and become frustrated. If you tell your friend the truth about your disinterest, then you are inviting problems. Your friend may think she isn't important enough to be penciled into your schedule. Stating your truth can easily be overcome with, "Oh you will be fine, come on!"

The general public will not accept the answer 'I don't want to do that.'. Oftentimes, that particular answer is the truth of why we don't want to accept an invitation for an activity. As a result, we replace the truth with a more acceptable reason we won't participate. The truth is perceived as not good enough.

63

We need to start an acceptance revolution of the truth being good enough. The truth is enough. You are enough. In a world of too much, you are enough.

Making the Right Decision

There is a lot of pressure to make the right decision. Some will lament a decision for days and weeks, sometimes longer in an effort to make the right choice. It really isn't that difficult. We either make the right decision, or we make the decision right. Either way, we are set up for success. We make the right decision. We make the decision right. Win/win. Don't sweat it. Just make your best choice. If the decision is right, then great! If not, then we make the decision right by changing things to accommodate that choice in life. An example would be quitting your job. It is either the right decision or not. If it is the right selection then we made the right decision. If it isn't the right selection then we make the decision right by not looking back, looking forward and doing the next right thing to move forward. That makes your decision to quit working the right choice either way. This methodology of making decisions moves us toward a more confident version of our authentic self and the fact that we are "enough" because there is a lot of peace in knowing you can't make a bad decision.

Desire Trumps Talent

I am a jack of all trades and a master of none. I have always been able to do anything I put my mind to and do a good job of it. Maybe not a perfect job, but a good job is something I can do. I have learned in my life that someone who wants to do something will do a better job than someone who does the same job with more talent but no desire.

Desire trumps talent every day and twice on Sunday. Think about it. If you want to build a desk but you don't know how, you will look up every YouTube video and read every book imaginable that will show you how to build that desk exactly as you want it. You will go out and buy the tools, read the directions, and work hard at the end goal, a desk. When your desk is finished it will look amazing because you had the desire to learn to do it. You may not have had natural ability to build a desk, but your desire to do it allowed you to study hard and learn from those who have gone before you.

The opposite scenario: You have to build a desk because you can. You will lament the fact that you are having to build it in the first place, dislike every moment of the process, and go through the motions to complete the task. Now from those two scenarios, whose desk is better? Desire trumps talent every time. The guy who wanted to build the desk did a better job than the guy with talent who did not want to do it.

It is the same situation with my Bible teaching discussed earlier. Those who wanted to teach

Bible class did a better job than I did because they wanted to do the teaching. I had the skills to teach but didn't do a very good job because I did not like it.

This line of thinking makes us more authentic because we learn that wanting to do something is more important than having a particular ability to do that same something. It takes the pressure off of us. We don't have to say to ourselves that we can't do something. If we WANT to do something then we will do a better job than someone who has the natural talent to do said thing. Wanting to do a task is enough. It is enough to complete the task and do a stellar job at it. Desire is enough. You are enough.

Not Everyone Will Like You

We were all made in God's image and all with different abilities, appearances and personalities. Think how vanilla the world would be if we were all alike. And on the same hand, think how the world would be if everyone were like me. Bless. Help us all if everyone were like me. I am sure in your life you have met people that you just don't care for. I don't know that there has ever been a person in my life that I hated, hate is a very strong word, but definitely I have had people I didn't like.

I was not popular in high school. I remember one time sitting in my car before going into school thinking to myself, "I wonder why people don't like me. I am a pretty cool person and I have neat thoughts on things but people don't like me." Now remember, this was high school so take that thought process accordingly. Once I got out of high school and into college everyone liked me. That was college so take that thought process accordingly also. What did people see in me in college that high school kids didn't see in me then? And now that I am 49, what are you all seeing in me that people then did not see? It is interesting to me how this progression has manifested itself.

I think the key to acceptance is maturity. In high school we are trying to create some sort of pecking order in life. Why we do that, I do not know. What I do know is that it excludes a lot of people. Only a few people achieve top pecking order and those people I would dare say, do not think they achieved top pecking order either. So in high school, we are all just a melting pot of folks who are trying to find their way. Some are definitely nicer than others on that journey.

After wisdom enters and age creeps up, I came to the striking realization that not everyone is going to like me and that is ok. Not everyone is going to like you and that is ok also. This is important in realizing that you are enough in a world that is too much. Not even all family members are going to like you. AND THAT IS OK. Our worth is not dependent upon people who are blood, friends, acquaintances or people we meet on the street each day. Our worth is in Jesus Christ and Him crucified. So let me say this loudly so the folks in the back can hear me-YOU ARE ENOUGH even though some people won't like you. Everyone does not like everyone they meet. You don't, I don't, none of us do. So because someone does not like you does not mean you could or should do something to MAKE them like you. You are enough in a world of too much. Don't worry about those that don't like you, move along. There are enough people who do like you that we need not worry about those who don't.

You Won't Like Everyone

You are not going to like everyone and that is ok. I have actually spent some time in my life feeling bad about the fact that I just don't particularly care for some people. I not sure where I got that crazy idea, but one fine day I woke up and decided that it was ok that everyone was not my cup of tea. This decision released the pressure and moved me a step closer to my authentic self.   I will be too much for some people.   They are not my people.   I am enough, and in being enough, there will be some people that I just don't care for. Release yourself.

Doing What We Do

Do you have any idea why we do what we do? Why do we get up in the morning? Why do we cook dinner at night? Why do we eat out every night? Why do we watch the news at 6pm? We do what we do because it is what we did yesterday. Think about that. We are all creatures of habit. Habits are never broken or disposed of. Habits are simply replaced by other habits. For example, I used to drink diet coke all day long every day. I decided that it was affecting my memory upon research on the subject of artificial sweeteners. I decided that I needed to quit drinking them but I like them so much that I made a choice to allow myself one diet coke per day. I replaced the rest of my diet coke for the day with water. I did not quit drinking, I just replaced my diet coke with water. I drank diet coke all day because it was what I did yesterday. Now I drink one diet coke and water the rest of the day. Same habit, different drink. We do what we do because it was what we did yesterday. Understanding why we do what we do helps us morph into our authentic selves and realize that we are enough.

In the South, Everything is a Coke

When my son was a toddler, he did not need to talk because his sister talked for him. She would walk in the kitchen with him on her hip and say, "He wants a cookie" and he got a cookie. No need for him to speak. When he did start talking, he had trouble pronouncing the hard C. We were at my mom's house and my Boy wanted a coke. He said to my mom, "I want a toke". Momma proceeded to correct him twice and say, "Say C C C Coke". My Boy said, "I want a Dr. Pepper."

Be an Electric Skillet

If you want to fry some southern food, you need an electric skillet. Cast iron skillets are good for many things, especially cornbread but if I am frying chicken, an electric skillet is key. In a regular frying pan on the stovetop, the heat is not distributed evenly. There are hot spots and warm spots no matter how particular you are. Electric skillets distribute the heat evenly throughout the cookware. This is a good analogy to life.

We don't want to be a frying pan. We don't want to let life burn us up in one part and not heat us at all in another part. We want to be an electric skillet. We want to be even keeled, balanced, weight of our world distributed evenly throughout. Living a balanced life is so important. Do everything in moderation. In a frying pan life, we are yo yo dieting, losing and gaining. In a frying pan, we are mad or happy. In a frying pan, we are wishy washy and indecisive. In an electric skillet, we are decisive. We are eating everything in moderation. We are settled and content knowing that there are going to be highs and lows in life. Work on balance. Be an electric skillet. In a world of frying pans, be an electric skillet. The more you move from the frying pan into the electric skillet, the closer you are to your authentic self. Electric skillets are enough. You are enough. In a world of too much, you are enough.

Write a Different Story

I once heard someone say, "I don't ever say anything that isn't positive about my children while they are with me". This sort of idealism is contributing to the "participation trophy" mentality of society today. I raised my children differently. I raised them to understand that moms need other mom friends to talk about motherhood with or we will go crazy. I never hesitated to tell my best friend that my son failed algebra and I also didn't hesitate to tell her that he went door to door during the flood to help rescue trapped homeowners. I always told my children, "If you don't like what I am saying then write a different story for yourself". They were raised to know that I am going to discuss what they did well, and I am also going to discuss what they did that wasn't so good if I need to vent or get some advice. My children know how important is is to not be alone with your thoughts. They realize that we all need to vent to trusted individuals. If they stole a pencil at school, they know I may discuss that with a friend while they are standing there. Moms of all ages, we need each other. Raising kids is not for the faint of heart and if we don't vent to one another about what our kids have done, good and bad, then we risk isolation and fears that we are alone. Let's not raise a generation of snowflakes. Let's raise our children to be strong, integrity filled contributors to society who understand that none of us are going to get out of here alive so we hold hands and stick together. And if you don't like what mom is saying about you, write a different story for yourself.

This mentality breeds authenticity into your children at an early age. Authenticity at its core promotes the fact that none of us are perfect. We all make mistakes. To be fully authentic, we admit our faults into audiences who may need to hear our story to help foster a feeling of solidarity. If we start our children out hearing their faults and their achievements being verbalized to others with the purpose of promoting solidarity and helping others to not feel alone, then they are a step ahead of the pansies who are sheltered from everyday life and only faced with positive reinforcement. Don't get me wrong, I am a fan of positive reinforcement, but balanced with some reality that we are all a hot mess. Some just hide it better than others. This mentality also shows children that they are enough. With all their good and bad, they are enough.

Bag of Faults

None of us are perfect. Each one of us has a collection of faults that we parade around or try to tweak and improve on a daily basis. I always gave a name to this as "Bag of Faults". Everyone has a bag of faults and when it comes time to find a mate, we find someone with a bag of faults that we can live with. Some people can live with someone who is an alcoholic, so marrying someone who is addicted would not be a big deal. To others, alcoholism is a fault in the bag that would be a deal breaker. Some people cannot stand messy people so if you are messy then you would not be a good candidate to marry. For others, it does not matter if you leave your clothes all over the house and leave the kitchen a mess.

When we detect that everyone has a bag of faults, we are able to discern that we are enough, even with our own bag of faults. I am enough.

The Bachelor/Bachelorette

My kids never have dated many people and I am good with that. I raised them to understand that dating was useful to find someone who has a bag of faults that you can live with. If you can weed out people without dating them then that is all the better as far as I am concerned. There are just too many things that can go wrong with dating in this day and time in my opinion. Everyone is entitled to my opinion.

There has always been controversy surrounding the long running show The Bachelor/Bachelorette. I actually used to enjoy the show(not so much anymore) and would invite my children to watch it with me. We used the show as a learning tool for dating. We would look at the faults of the contestants and discuss what we could and could not live with. Even if the girl or guy was portrayed to be someone she was not in real life, it still was a teaching tool for me as a mother to be able to discuss behaviors in people that we like or don't like. Using this show has helped narrow down the dating field for my children without having to engage with a particular person. Call it odd if you want to, but it worked for us and has maintained a level of purity in my children that may have been sacrificed if they had dated the masses in person. This practice also helped identify authentic qualities in my children so they were on the fast track to being who they are without having to impress society with trying to fit in. Think about it. It was almost like a virtual dating world for my kids.

What is Wrong

Whatever is wrong in your life this very minute is just a small bleep on the radar of eternity. Read that again.

Help Someone Today

When your feet hit the floor each morning, make it your goal to help someone today. We all need help. It may be help carrying something. It may be a listening ear. It may be advice on a business idea. It may be opening a door. Whatever small thing you can do to help someone today, do it. Make someone's day by helping them today. Blow their pool float up with your compressor. Make them dinner. Take their baby while they take a nap. Help someone. Be like Nike, Just do it. I promise you will be the one who is blessed and you will find that your small act of kindness will show you that you are enough. In a world of too much, you are enough.

Decorate your Disaster

Many times in life, there is disaster. It may be in the form of death, unemployment, or divorce. Whatever it is, it can be a big green monster in the room everywhere you go. My husband was unemployed for 14 months in 2009-2011. He has always been a road warrior. When the economy tanks, the sales guys are always the first to be cut back in corporations. I was a stay at home mom. My husband and I had the best times while he was unemployed. We spent a lot of time together, enjoyed each other's company, did things together, learned to have fun with no money again like we did when we were first married, etc. It was a good time. Let me be real here, it was tough too. The self esteem my husband lost was no joke. Getting his job taken away was a blow to his ego big time. Each day when we got up, I felt like there was this big green monster living in our home that we tried to avoid and not discuss. After about a month or so with this big green monster called unemployment, we decided we would decorate it and splash some greenery on it so that it blended better with our family. It wasn't so intrusive and abrasive when it was decorated.

We had a family meeting and exposed this big green monster called Unemployment. We decided that we all would add some decoration to it so that we could live with it while it was here. Greenery was big in homes at the time, ficus trees, etc, so I threw some hypothetical greenery on Unemployment. My husband let it hold his golf clubs. Our children played games with it and invited it to play Barbies and swing on the swing set.

Unemployment, divorce, or any tragedy does not have to be as invasive as we can allow it to be. We can accept that it is here for a bit, decorate our disaster and make it comply with our family dynamics until it goes away. At that time, we can drop kick it out the door. Even in hard times, we are enough and no tragedy has the right to destroy our world if we don't want it to. It can make us stronger and more authentic.

Learn Something New Every Day

Did you know that there are actually people out there who do not want to learn anything else? That BLOWS my mind. I am SO not like that. I am a lifelong learner. I have met people who do not want to gain further knowledge. Many times, they come across as know it alls, don't want to hear other people's opinions because they think they already know it. I actually keep my thoughts to myself many times in public just because I want to hear what other people think or believe because I am open minded. I make it my goal each day to learn something new. It helps me be my authentic self.

Go out today and learn something new , then acknowledge that it as such. I say at least once a week, "I learn something new every day."

I especially enjoy new vocabulary. I suppose that writers and readers enjoy new words. Here is a fun fact: If you learn a new vocabulary word, then use it in context 10 times the day that you learn it and it will become a part of your normal conversation. True fact. Try it.

Don't Look Back

Never look back in regret. Every decision you make along your life's journey was exactly what you wanted or had to do at the time. It was the best choice at that very moment in time. Regret will eat you up. Don't look back, we aren't going that way. We are going forward and the sooner you are able to realize that and accept it, the sooner you will adopt the fact that you are enough. Whatever decision you made was enough. You did what you thought best. We use what we know at the time to make decisions that are best. We are moving onward. You are enough. In a world of too much, you are enough.

Starting a Blog and the First Glimpses of the Reporter in Me

{Backstory - This was my first post, copied word for word from my original blog. Before I started doing videos, I began my reporting by referring to myself as Barbara Walters, then giving the live report. This entry is included because it gives prophecy of the book you are reading now.}

Barbara Walters here reporting live from the Blogging World where Jennifer Anglin has created a Blog. Folks, trust me, she has no CLUE what she is doing but here she goes. It took her 4 days to even come up with a name for such a thing as a blog. What in the world IS a blog? WHO would even read one? Well, apparently, Jennifer has been told by one too many people to start a blog or write a book that the blog has been created. The book is still in the computer, and is still being worked on, slowly but surely in between making laundry detergent and making a massive mutiny against excess in the home.

Interestingly enough, Points to Ponder was considered as the blog name. Points to Ponder is a term that I used to use when I was a wee one just in high school when I would come up with a thought. I would state my thought and follow it up with "Now that is a Point to Ponder". Would you believe that is already taken as a blog name? What in the world? Do these people not realize that I have mentally copyrighted that term? When I googled who had the site, it had not been updated since 2007. What? Shouldn't there be an auto delete option for non-use, especially when I want to resurrect the name?

{Ultimately I used the name Fun Thoughts on Life, the Weather, and All Things Groovy as the name of my blog and it has served me well. This next entry was also included in that first blog post}

Epiphany of Motherhood

Today I reached the epiphany of my motherhood. Yes, I said it. Epiphany of Motherhood. My youngest daughter and I were cleaning out her room and I asked her to go downstairs to get the Magic Eraser. The following conversation ensued:

Daughter: What is a magic eraser?

Me: It is that white block under the kitchen sink that looks kinda like a sponge.

97

Daughter: OH and you wet it?

Me: Yes, wet it and then wring it out good and bring it up here and wipe the spots off your walls.

Daughter: Ok
(thundering elephant down the stairs, slam cabinet, water full force, thundering elephant up the stairs)

Me: Now wipe the spots on the wall

Daughter: OH LOOK AT THIS! It is getting all this marker and stuff off the wall!

Me: Yes, it is, It is a Magic Eraser.

Daughter: This is so COOL!

For at least an hour after that, my youngest went about the entire house finding everything in sight that she could clean with the magic eraser. She cleaned so many things that, had I asked her to clean, would have never gotten cleaned. But because of the introduction of the Magic Eraser, somehow cleaning was fun today. Epiphany. Chances are, this will never happen again, but today, I will take it, and be very grateful for the help. And that, my friends, is a Point to Ponder.

Caring For Others-If you Aren't in the Freezer, Then You are Doing Just Fine

How Are You? It is a question asked all too often by folks just making conversation. Do we really want to know how someone is? If we don't then we should come up with a larger vocabulary of "niceties" to exchange. Like maybe "Good to see you today". Unless we really DO want to know, hear, and have the time to listen. The world would be a better place if we all took time to exchange enough transparency to ask with integrity, How are you? We should be able to share a transparent answer or have time to listen with empathy. Now that, my friends, is a point to ponder.

On the subject of How Are You?, I bring your attention to my good friend Iris. Iris is an

Emu. Sadly, Iris has never been featured as one of the most fascinating people. Though not a "people", she really is. Iris's home is in Chicago, Illinois. She lives on a farm there with some horses, too many roosters and hens to count, a donkey, and a plethora of other animals. In recent years, I have had the pleasure of visiting Iris each summer. When we pull up in the driveway, my best friend, her aunt, and our children will go over to the fence, start calling for Iris and she will start thumping. An Emu's natural noise sounds like a drum. A BIG BASS DRUM. It is the oddest sound I have ever heard. Iris generally hides in the brush, but when we call her, she thumps and then ambles over and peeks out from the tall grass. This past summer when my friend and I went to Chicago, we left the children at home because we were going to see a Woman about a Horse. When we arrived at Iris' home,

I got out and went by myself to call for her. She came right over and sat down and let me sit down beside her. It was hilarious when I got out my Iphone and was trying to take pictures of the two of us together. It was as though Iris was smiling. She likes to wear a birthday hat at parties. She has quite a personality. The farm only has one Emu. I asked the owner of the farm why Iris was the only Emu and their answer was this simple: "Well, we did not intend to have Iris, but we recognized quickly that she was quite the entertainer so we decided to keep her here on the farm. Her brothers and sisters are in the freezer." My friends, when asked how you are doing each day, the answer is as simple as Iris the Emu. If you are not in the freezer you are doing just fine! Iris was enough and so are you. In a world of too much, YOU are enough.

Be Yourself, Everyone Else is Taken

Elementary, Middle, High School, even College...I spent these times trying to walk, talk, and be like someone else. Someone I viewed as popular, I wanted to walk like them, or hold my books like they do when they walk down the hall. I wanted to fix my hair like they did and it never seemed to work out because in my adult life I learned that different hair textures just won't go into certain styles. Explains why we have those "awkward years" where we all look a bit like animals at the zoo. However, there is always that set of animals or even one animal that we want to look or be like trying to emulate them at all costs. Even growing up we try to be like our parents and fit into their mold. Then when we get out on our own we still carry that mold with us and our first meals we cook are the meals we had at home(even though they aren't worth eating at that time because they aren't as good as what momma made). The truth of the matter is, when we try to be like everyone else, we feel trapped, like we are put into a box and it becomes claustrophobic.

For me, the real transformation to being myself came about 15 years ago when I decided to cut my hair into the spiky do. I remember at the time I was working part time at the bank and I mentioned to a couple of my co-workers that I wanted to get my hair cut spiky. Of course, I met with protest. Oh NO, you don't want to cut your hair like that! Well, maybe I do. YOU may not want to cut YOUR hair like that, but maybe I do. It took me another month or two before I was brave enough to cut it because I have to admit, it is SO hard to overcome people's opinions and when they seem to be free flowing, it makes it even harder. I did cut my hair and I have had it like it is now, spiky and sassy, ever since. I am fairly convinced that I will never have another hairdo. It suits me perfectly. It is ME. Anyone who knows me knows that it is ME. I feel so free. If we all could take a step back and realize that everyone is different, and not to impose our opinions upon other people then there would be a lot less pressure and stress in the world today. Embrace our differences. If you are out with a friend and she says, how do you like this shirt? Say, That would look great on you! Trying to make other people fit into molds is one of the most debilitating habits that has been presented into our world today. Embrace yourself. Be yourself, Because everyone else is taken. Now that is a point to ponder.

This very point is the reason that dieting never works. Every diet tries to put us into a mold that we don't fit into. Diets try to make us eat foods that we don't normally eat or don't normally like. God made us all different and some of us don't like plain yogurt and blueberries. Some of us like chocolate and pizza. And some of us want to be healthy and thin.

See if you recognize this pattern: Decide to diet, go on the diet, buy the foods suggested, stick to it for a week or two or a month or two, loose some weight, get excited, stick to it another week or two, feel deprived, binge, go back to what you were doing before, gain the weight back plus some extra.

In my experience with dieting, the reason this happens is simple: we were trying to be someone else. We can't be someone else, because someone else is already taken, we must be ourselves. Folks, the secret to healthy dieting and weight loss is simple: Eat what you want, just not a lot of it. That way, we are being ourselves, and we are setting ourselves up for success instead of failure. If I want a piece of pie, I eat one, but a very small piece. When you go to a restaurant, ask for a to go box when your meal arrives and put half of it in the box. No one needs the absurd portion that is presented at a restaurant. Order what you want, just don't eat all of it. This way you are not depriving yourself. The #1 reason that we don't stick to diets is because we get sick of depriving ourselves of things we love and we cave in. And when we have deprived ourselves for so long, heaven help the first pie we dive into... If we eat what we want, just not a lot of it, then we are not depriving ourselves. We are cutting calories without deprivation. Can you live the rest of your life without pie or carbohydrates? NO, Can you live the rest of your life eating what you want in small quantities? YES! Yes we can! Setting ourselves up for success we are!

Fat Burning

NOW! Finally I am going to share the secret to fat burning. I wish I had known this before now lest I would not have spent my life overweight. I figured out the problem.

When you use shampoo in the shower the suds run all down your body. You can't help but let the suds run. I read on the bottle of shampoo, and they all say it no matter what kind you use, "Adds volume and extra body" This has been the problem all along. My shampoo running down my body has been adding extra body and volume making me fat all my life. Well, I have a solution for us. I started washing my hair in Dawn dishwashing liquid. On the label it reads, "Dissolves Fat that is otherwise Hard to Remove" Problem solved! And it is great for oily hair.

Witnessing a Modern Day Miracle and Realization of Dreams

Let me start by saying that I have finally been granted permission by my oldest daughter to share her story. It is a beautiful story that God wrote from the very beginning. It has many gorgeous details and a lot of heartache. It is a story of perseverance, the triumph of the human spirit, never backing down, and most importantly, following God when the way seems dark and lonely and you can't see a light at the end of the tunnel. I am beyond delighted to have permission to write her story. It is my prayer as I candidly type her story that it will give even one person hope for another day.

My oldest daughter was about to turn 18 in a few short weeks. She was about to be graduating high school and attending college in the fall. When she was born, I had so many hopes and dreams for her like all moms do. I remember laying on the bed with her when she was a few days old and crying because I wanted her to be able to remain so innocent the rest of her life. I knew the world was cruel and I just ached for what she would experience and see in this world one day. I knew I couldn't save her from everything, but I vowed to that baby that I would die trying. It is a vow I have kept to my beautiful girl.

Fast forward to school days: Every mom gets excited and sad when their child goes off to Kindergarten, and every mom just knows that their kid is the smartest, the most adorable, etc. Up until they go to Kindergarten they

ARE! Then, all of the sudden, they are judged on the world's scale in school and it isn't always as pretty as we dreamed it to be. If you have a child that makes straight A's all the time and work is simple for them, I am so incredibly happy for you. I no longer wish that was my lot in life for motherhood. I am grateful for every tear that was shed over homework and every mean thing that has been said to my girl because this is God's story and my girl has turned into an incredibly hard worker, self motivated, Christian young lady who will do amazing things in God's kingdom in her life. I spent many years crying and praying that things be easier for my girl. Praise God that He said, "No".

Fast Forward to 2nd Grade: Having had a terrible time in school and grades that suffered, we began to believe there was a

113

problem. We took her to have her eyes tested and her hearing tested. We ultimately had testing done through the school and pediatrician where the diagnosis was Attention Deficit Disorder and a learning disability. NOT what I dreamed of when my girl was born. We moved on, and things improved with knowledge of how to deal with our daughter. A behavioral therapist was involved and also was able to help us tremendously to teach our daughter how to deal with her "lot".

Kids are mean and there have been many hurtful things uttered to our girl about being dumb and stupid and "special ed". I can't believe that special ed is actually a term children use to refer to another one of God's creatures. In our home, we celebrate D's if we worked hard to get them. ABCDF are letters used to judge knowledge on the world's scale, NOT GOD'S SCALE. God's scale judges how much character a child has, and how loving they are, and whether or not they are kind to one another. My girl is all of these things.

In 6th grade, there was new legislation that allowed a child to receive special education services for medical reasons such as Attention Deficit Disorder as well as learning disability. We made a very hard decision to place her in that program so she could receive the best education opportunity offered. In the meantime, I prayed daily for my girl that things be easier for her and many other specifics as they arose. Also in the meantime, she grew to love the Lord even more, she grew in stature, faith and in favor with God and man. She learned to work circles around the other "smarter" kids in class, learned to be incredibly organized, and learned to develop tough skin for hurtful words from mean kids and teasing that was not intended to be teasing but was hurtful even from her best friends.

Fast forward to12th grade: She was accepted to college by the grace of God based on her grades which was a feat orchestrated entirely by the one and only God. Her grade point average continued to rise, provisions were taken away gradually as we learned to learn. Ultimately in the 11th and 12th grade, all special education provisions were removed and my girl was allowed to spread her wings and fly. She received her first set of straight A's. We all cried and celebrated because we knew that she had finally proved on the *world's scale* just once that she was smart, a quality that we knew she was all along, but

now the world had proof.   TAKE THAT
world!

We had to go to the pediatrician to get booster
shots for college and per the checkup
protocol, a hearing test which she failed
miserably. We have had hearing tests almost
yearly and she never had passed one, even
when we took her to Bill Wilkerson Hearing
Institute at Vanderbilt when she was 10. It
was always treated with antibiotics
and antihistamines to remove fluid, repair
burst ear drum, or some other
medical anomaly that may have been present
in her ears at the time.   Our pediatrician
referred her to an audiologist and a doctor of
facial and head surgery to be evaluated for
hearing. We attended the appointment where
we were told that our daughter had "severe
hearing loss". The doctor continued to talk

and I began to cry not because he told me my daughter needed hearing aids, but because he told our entire story in the context of her hearing loss and he had never met us before to know the struggles our child had in school. All these things were related to hearing loss and not Attention Deficit Disorder OR a learning disability. The child simply could not hear.

Now, many would be furious, but not me. No sir! We can't look back we can only look forward, and praise God that we found this! Had God intended us to find out this problem before now, He would have let it be known and her failed hearing tests would not have been dismissed as fluid, ear infection, etc.

I witnessed a miracle. I praise God and thank Him tearfully that I was able to witness His miracle. We went to the Audiologist who fitted my girl with hearing aids. They were programmed to her hearing loss via computer and placed in her ears.

My girl was literally giddy when she heard for the first time. She got very teary eyed because she was hearing for the very first time in her life. She started laughing and listening. The audiologist said, "Go outside and ask her a question without her being able to see you" My girl said, "I heard that!" She rubbed the chair arm that I was sitting in and pulled her hand away like she touched something hot and I asked her what was wrong, and she said, "Oh my goodness, did you hear that? The chair arm makes noise when you rub it!" She proceeded to tap, whistle and laugh a lot. I looked over at her because she was making so much noise I couldn't hear the audiologist.

She said, "I am just enjoying hearing!" Our moments since then have involved her self discovery of the world of hearing. It is something we take for granted every day. I will not take this for granted ever again. It has been a wonderful time to watch how excited she is about every noise that I never think about but that she has never heard. She texted me the very next day from school and said she said the pledge that day. She had not heard it before.

I am so grateful that God chose me to be this fabulous girl's mother. She has taught me more about life than I would ever have learned from anywhere else. I am also grateful that God chose to write this wonderful story for my girl and for all the heartache that goes with it, for it made her what she is today: perfect! She went on to graduate college in 2018 and is very successful in her job.

It has been hard for her to adjust to the world of hearing. She goes through long periods of time where she refuses to wear her hearing aids because they bother her and she does not like to hear all the time. It was quiet in her world and she does not always like the noise of life. She reads lips incredibly well. If you met her, you may never even know that she can't hear.

Interestingly enough, the doctor said that because she was the first born, and because I am a loud person and was a stay at home mother, my daughter never developed a speech impediment that goes stereotypically with hearing issues. If I were to bear my soul, this is the only fact in this story that redeemed my "momma heart". I felt like the worst mother on the planet for not catching this myself. At least, my being a loud person benefitted something in my life. My girl doesn't have a speech problem because I am loud. It took me a while to work through my own guilt about these events but this is a large part of what catapulted me to be my authentic self. In the end, I resigned myself that as her mother, I was enough. I was enough for her, even with my flaws. I knew that I was an attentive mother, and if God wanted me to know that she had a hearing problem, He had plenty of chances to reveal that because she had great doctor care and even had her hearing evaluated at a very prestigious hospital in Nashville. I am enough. In a world of too much, I am enough.

Don't Major in Minors

If God can part the Red Sea to allow Moses and the Egyptians to cross on dry land, then He can SURELY place a mouse in a car.

This story is a real eye opener to not major in minors. My dad, who is my biggest fan, the man who is my first love, who never acted annoyed by my presence no matter how busy he was when I was growing up, the one who loves me unconditionally and is the embodiment of my "glass half full" attitude, had been in the hospital with a life threatening problem. When a doctor says to you, "Your dad could bleed to death in less than a minute. He needs life saving surgery.", you sit up and take notice real quick.

Apparently, not majoring in minors is a lesson much needed in the Anglin home because God taught it to us in a most unusual way:

The Setting: the car

The Problem: A protein bar that had been opened but not visibly eaten

The Story: A protein bar was stored in the car for lunch one day. When it was decided to be eaten, it was discovered that the package had been opened and when reached for, crumbs sprinkled all over. A call was received at the hospital while my dad was in a serious condition to explain the opened and partially eaten bar.   The call was very quickly dispelled, upon frustration with such a minor problem being addressed during a grave situation. Not happy with no solution to the much important protein bar, more family were called and questioned about the protein bar.

Upon arriving home, the bar was produced and shown to the family and the questioning continued since no perpetrator had been found. I picked up the Protein Bar and immediately saw the problem. There was no way that a human had opened, much less eaten this bar. The teeth marks were way too tiny and the packaging had been chewed off and some was missing. (Another case solved by the FBI agent in the home) It was then stated that the "crumbs that scattered from the package were possibly not crumbs at all.

The Conversation:

Anglin A-Who ever heard of a mouse in a car? And how could a mouse even get in a car?

Anglin B-If God could part the Red Sea for Moses and the Egyptians to walk across on dry land, then I am certain He could place a mouse in a car to teach us what is important in life.

The Plan:
Set a mouse trap in the car with a piece of protein bar as bait.

The Resolution: The mouse was caught in the trap...in the car. Craziest thing ever.

The Lesson: Don't major in minors.

Folks, lets all take a step back and realize what is important in life: God, Family and Friends-all people. Not protein bars, not stuff, just people. Now that is a point to ponder.

Teen Dating: I am not Always Convinced We will Survive Raising the Children

All I ever wanted to be was a mother. I played with dolls until, well, I still do. People crack me up that say, "My child will NEVER do that." Or "If my child did that or acted like that I would wear them out and they would never do that again." Well, good luck with all of that. I hope that you are more successful with those words than I was.

I remember being in college and dreaming of what I would name my children someday. I would have 6 because I did not want my children to be only children like I am. Some of the ones I remember were Kyler and Kaylor. They were going to be twins. Heaven help me if I had actually birthed twins. I would have had to raise them. Two in diapers, two to buy baby food for, two to date, bury me now. Yes, adorable they would have been, but a lot of work they would also have been. Although the truth of the matter is that I would have done a great job raising Kyler and Kaylor and their 4 brothers and sisters had God had that in my life plans. God had the perfect plan for my life and my family.

[This story was written several years ago, so the ages noted below were the ages of our children at the time of this particular entry]

My husband and I have three beautiful children. The oldest is a girl, a most precious love who is truly a gift from God, and is almost 18, graduating from high school this year. Our middle child is a boy, our only boy, and most special boy, who is 14. Our youngest is a girl, age 10, and she is our Frosting, our sweetness, our baby. And then there is Zoe, our dog, who is almost 1 and had I known a dog was so great, may have had her first and left the other three off the list of family members based on their behavior on any given day. We planned our children 4 years apart so that we did not "boot anyone out of the nest" for the next baby to come along. It was a fabulous plan, and one that worked perfectly for us. We never experienced any jealously when we brought a new baby home. Yes, we had some incidents, but overall, the older child, or children were excited to have the new baby to come home with us.

Thanks to the good Lord, I have been able to stay at home with the children for most of their growing up thus far. I do think it makes a difference in the children when you are available for them. I know many working moms who are able to do both beautifully. I admire you tremendously.

Here is a thought that I have discovered is totally wrong: If we have to choose a time to be at home with the children, when they are babies is the most important time. Although this is a very important time, and you miss many firsts if you are unable to care for your children full time when they are babies, the truth of the matter is that anyone can feed them a bottle and change their diaper and talk to them. But when they get older, SOMEONE is going to influence them, and if you are not around and not readily available, YOU are not going to be the one that influences them. Thus, we need to be readily available physically, mentally, emotionally, and spiritually for our preteens and teens or they will be influenced by others and many times it won't be good. Be available.

Let's talk about dating. In my home, I introduced the concept of Contract Dating. Contract dating is basically this: If you want to date my daughter, we have rules, and you both may abide by them, or you will not be allowed to date.

Please fill out the paperwork, sign and date, and I hope you both have a joyful, well behaved date(and the car behind you is mine because this mother is better than any FBI agent ever dreamed of being). If you break the rules, you will be shown the door, thanks for playing.

Some of the rules in the paperwork are as follows:

1. You will not cover up with blankets.

2. You will sit up on the couch. (If you are too tired to sit up, then you should go home and sleep)

3. You will greet the adults in the home and carry on intelligent conversation with them.

4. You will not hit, kick, pinch, grab, or restrain my daughter in any way, shape, form, or fashion, even in a playful way because we do not find that behavior playful or amusing.

5. You will not download or listen to explicit music, videos, or media to our computers.

6. You will treat our daughter's brother and sister with respect and give them the time of day when they enter a room.

7. You will not touch the torso area of my daughter, and she will not touch you in the torso area.

8. You will only use Princess terminology when talking to my daughter. You will not use expletives, or any language that could be defined as orally abusive by the parents.

9. You will not use vulgarities in text, phone calls, or in person. If you are tempted to use such references, we will help you to broaden your vocabulary so that you can use other words that are less offensive.

10. You are not allowed to drive my daughter's car unless prior permission is given or blood is involved.

I have read and agree to the terms and conditions of dating the Anglin daughter. Any violation of these rules will result in immediate termination of the right to see her.

Signed_____

Date_____

Daughter_____

Date_____

The idea of contract dating has been very successful here in the Anglin Home. It has successfully rid us of a toxic boyfriend, and has also caused our daughter to be selective about who she dates because only the best kids would not be scared off by such a contract. I have found from experience, that children will rise to the occasion, and boys will comply if they know what you expect from the get go. Also, contract dating removes the blame from Mom and Dad. Your child and their boyfriend/girlfriend are in charge of their ability to date. They violate, its their own fault, not yours. They knew the rules and signed the paper.

Now THIS is a lot to ponder. Take heart, weary pilgrims, for if your children are small, at least you know where they are. They are right under your feet crying. When they get older, you are chasing them around to make sure they are doing the right things, OR, like most people, you are just burying your head in the sand and not paying attention to what your teens are doing. NOT GOOD! Don't even for a second believe that your child wouldn't do that. That is self fulfilling prophesy...They WILL do it. It is unusual if they don't. Look around at all the fine, church going people around, and even look at yourself. Did you behave like you would want your children to? Ok then. Take measures and chase your children. Become an FBI agent. Pray a LOT! It will save the children.

Mr. Clean

Mr. Clean created a handy little item called the Magic Eraser. It is a sponge of some sort that when dampened will wipe just about any blemish or mark from most anything. It can make the dirtiest of walls look new again, will take a little darling's masterpiece from the living room wall, take soap scum off of a shower door, remove mold and mildew and rust marks from porcelain and a host of other uses. No one really knows what is magic about Mr. Clean's eraser but it will even take permanent marker off of most things.

The original Magic Eraser rose from the tomb over 2,000 years ago. His resurrection has the ability to make the dirtiest of lives look new again. He can wipe any blemish or mark from anyone's life. He can remove a mess you made of your life that ruined your future. He can take scum and make it shiny and streak free. He can remove mold, mildew and rust from our lives that no amount of apologizing will erase. He can remove mistakes from our lives, even ones with permanent reminders.

Mr. Clean, although amazing, is not a new concept. My Mr. Clean died for my sins and rose again on the third day. My Mr. Clean is your Mr. Clean. We accept our Mr. Clean when we confess His name before men, and dampen ourselves in the burial waters of baptism. He then magically erases our mistakes, even ones with permanent reminders.

Because of Mr. Clean, we are enough. I am enough. You are enough.

137

Exposing Your Authentic Self

We all need to be authentic, be ourselves on a day to day basis. If you don't even know who you are that is a place to start. In my early adult life, I remember and even look back on pictures at how I dressed and how I did my hair and how I cooked and how I acted. It all was about what someone else thought I should wear, look like, act like, cook like, etc. I talked about my decision to cut my hair short and spiky and how I was met with much opposition in that decision. The bottom line there is that you may not want your hair short and spiky but I do. And that is ok. You may not want to wear black, but I do. You may not like to allow your children to get their cartilage pierced, but I choose not to fight that battle. The fact is that we are all different and God made us this way. We all need to be tolerant and accepting of other people's desires, opinions, style of dress, and ways to raise their children because what may be good for one person may not be good for another person. But we should be supportive of what other people like and do as long as it is not harmful or against God's word. What we don't realize is that our support of others relieves a ton of pressure to allow us all to be authentic. We are all human and as much as we would not like to let the opinions of others affect our decisions, the fact is that it does. So if we all would be in support of different people's different strategies to survive life, raising kids, and dressing themselves, then we would all feel much more free to be who we are. Let's face it, not everyone can just say , "Forget them, I am going to do what I want to do." So a little tolerance and keeping your

139

mouth shut with your opinions will help tremendously towards a birth of authenticism in everyone. Let's all take time to cut down the pressure by keeping our opinions to ourselves and only show support and not negativity unless it is harmful or against God's word, and your definition of harmful may not be really harmful in the grand scheme of things.

The reason people lie is because they believe the truth will not be good enough. Read that statement twice or three times. We discussed this statement in an earlier entry in this book. It is about as true as anything on this planet. One of the ways to be authentic is to tell the truth all the time and let that be good enough. When you realize that people lie because they believe the truth is not good enough then you can tell the truth all the time because your truth IS good enough. We all make mistakes and sometimes our truth is not pretty but it is part of the knitting of the fabric of our lives. If we are allowing ourselves to be authentic then we will admit that we are not perfect and tell of times when we made mistakes because God allows us to suffer to help others along the way. What I have been through may help someone else, but if I keep it to myself then who am I helping? I heard a story of Jews escaping concentration camps and the years of work they spent mapping and planning. Once they escaped do you think they kept their info to themselves? NO. They shared it so others could escape. If we are transparent and share our struggles with others then we are being authentic and you will find that others will come out of the woodwork showing gratitude for sharing because they have been closet sufferers of the same thing. Being Authentic means being transparent. No one is perfect and if you act like you are then you are living a lie. Your story can help others.

God's Timing Almost Always is not Our Timing

I went to a wedding. I have been to many weddings in my life, all of which have been beautiful. This particular night, I went to the most beautiful wedding I have ever been to not because the decorations were the best I had ever seen, or the bride looked the most beautiful, or the groom was the most handsome, or the weather was the most perfect, or the food was the best I had ever eaten. In fact, I really paid less attention to any of these physical properties than I have at any wedding I have ever been to. The wedding I went to that night was a culmination of God's perfect timing. It was the most beautiful event I have ever been to. There were no physical bridesmaids, or physical groomsmen. The witness that stood up with the bride and groom was the one and only God.

The bride's son sat on the front row along with the parents of both the bride and groom. There was not a dry eye in the audience. The groom and bride walked out of the back of the house and ambled hand in hand dripping with joy to the altar of greenery over an archway. God saw this day long ago and the happily ever after that it began for these two. God wiped their tears individually for the past years as the wounds were deep and raw from failed marriages and previous spouses who taught them who NOT to marry.

The bride was one of my best friends, not because we spent a lot of time together, that is not always necessary. We had been to hell and back together in different situations, but we put our backs together through the rain and slept that way so neither one of our heads fell in the mud. There has been a lot of mud for a lot of years. When my mud dried and I was able to walk on dry land again, my best friend continued to struggle. Some days we wondered if her misery would ever end. If it wasn't flies it was ants. But faithful love is a friend just when hope seems to end, welcome face, sweet embrace, tender touch filled with grace. Faithful love drowns each fear, reaches down, dries each tear, holds my hand when I can't stand on my own.

One day, a very handsome man who I have known my whole life and whose father was one of my Christian mentors growing up came in to Sunday school and sat next to my best friend. By the time Sunday school was over, he was practically sitting in her seat with her. Both happier than I had seen them in years. My husband and I elbowed each other and snickered to ourselves without saying a word. I couldn't tell you what that Bible class was about that day because I was watching what God was doing right in the row in front of me. That prince and princess were married at that wedding with God in attendance.

The wedding was perfect, the decorations were perfect, the bride was the most beautiful, the groom most handsome, the food the greatest I ever tasted, because God blessed the broken road that led them straight to paradise.

I was blessed to be able to witness the culmination of years of heartache that gave way to God's perfect plan, God's perfect timing, God's perfect family. It started to sprinkle rain during the ceremony, then it quit. It reminded me of how many tears my friend and I have dried for each other over the years. The rain stopped and so have the tears. If ever there was a happily ever after, this is it.

For my Friend's Prince Charming, she is enough. He is enough. They are enough. In a world of too much, they are enough.

Ways to Get Your Children Talking to You

Don't you just love it when you go to the dentist and the Doc or hygienist tries to talk to you while you have your mouth wide open and they are scraping crust from your teeth and the suction is halfway down your throat? Our children's version of this scenario is this: Don't you just love it when you are in the middle of your favorite show, or playing with your favorite toy, or trying to get ready to go out with your friends, or getting ready for school and your parents come in and try to talk to you? Timing is everything to get your children to talk and tell you the important stuff.

I am one very blessed momma in that my children tell me just about everything. Yes, they lie sometimes and yes, I have had some times that they have been doing things they shouldn't, but for the most part, they tell me stuff that I need to know. It is because I have set up open lines of communication from the very beginning. Showing your children that you are not going to panic or interrupt when they talk is important to establishing lines of communication. Remember when your kids fell and you give this look of horror to them and they start crying? I always have a pleasant look on my face when something happens and don't panic. That way the child can decide if it is an instance that warrants upset reaction. Don't panic, and look pleasant. Rule #1 to open lines of communication. If you start this early then not only will you establish credibility and openness with your little ones, it will train you to not panic so when they are teens and come to you with who had drugs at the party or who is trying to have sex with them then you won't panic either. I assure you your teens will not open up if you panic every time they speak to you about stuff.

When you go get your nails or hair done, it seems to be a time to talk to the person doing your nails or hair. I noticed this anomaly and the fact that at a hair salon, dirty laundry is hung without inhibition for all to hear. Cool!

I brought this home and used it on my children with much success. Regularly paint and clip your girl's nails and do their hair and the dirty laundry is out to dry. With my boy, it involves clipping and digging dirt. They don't realize that I have a motive in my pampering, but that is ok. I start out just like a hairdresser

150

does. What can I do for you today? What has been going on with you since the last time we did your nails, etc. My children have responded beautifully to this tactic. I get a lot of information out of them this way, and gives me a chance to listen to them. Again, don't panic, and don't ask too many questions. Over time, it establishes communication lines for anything, not just the easy stuff like where are we going to eat Friday night.

With my boy, shooting hockey is a good time to talk. Shoot hockey with him, shoot basketball with him, dig a hole in the yard with him, dig dirt out of his fingernails for him, all of which have been successful talking times for me with my boy. Again, don't panic or ask too many questions.

Bath time is a good time to talk when your children are small. My children used to tell me all kinds of things from bath time. However, I never panicked, offered too much advice, or looked shocked by anything they told me even from a young age.

What do I do if my child tells me something they did that is bad? You said not to panic! Well, I am glad you asked. The way I handle this is simple. I put it back on them. I say, "What do you think God is saying about what you are doing?" For me, it works every time. Gives them a chance to think through what happened, and how they should correct themselves. No shouting, no fussing, just correction. Children want to do what is right.

When they come home from school is a terrible time to talk, but it also is the best time to talk if you know what questions to ask. Here is the scenario: They get off the bus, come in the house, and you say Hey! How was school today? You are setting yourself up for closed lines of communication here. What is the answer to the overused "How was school today?" ? Well, it is "fine". Door shut, communication stunted, tv on, snack prepared, you are DONE momma! Try this and see if it doesn't get you further than a standard "fine". When my kids come home I say to them, Well you look happy today! or Well you look upset about something. or You look like you are excited about something. These comments open the door for a more thorough explanation or answer than "fine". Kids will correct you if you say they look happy and they are not at all! They will reply with No, I am not happy at all, I failed the math test and my best friend is saying I'm not her friend anymore. NOW, you lines are open and you can have a nice discussion of things. It is all in the questions you ask, folks, and asking the right questions opens the gates for our children to become their authentic selves and shows them that they are enough. You are enough. In a world of too much, you are enough.

Never Take Things for Granted

Barbara Walters here reporting live from the world of hearing! I am thrilled again to have been given permission to share these stories. My oldest daughter has actually asked me to include all of her discoveries about the world of hearing. She didn't have to ask me twice because it was such an exciting few days since she got her hearing aids which are called her "little miracles". Some of the items that she has learned about the world of hearing she thought were embarrassing, but now she sees the potential of how many could be impacted by her story that she wants to share more.

I must say that I have learned SO much in the past days about not taking things for granted. Sounds that I have not paid attention to ever, have been brought to my attention as my girl has heard them for the first time. I had to take my youngest to the pediatrician and everyone was interested in my story which I was incredibly thrilled to tell. Our doctor barely began to make mention of a "shoulda, coulda, woulda" thought that he had since finding out about my girl and her new life. I stopped him before he could even get started because this is God's story and not ours. God did what he wanted to do with my girl and I wouldn't change a thing. When you go to a Christian pediatrician, those conversations about what could have been different are not productive. We can't go back, only forward

You grow through what you go through.

Be thankful for the bad things in life. For they opened your eyes to the good things you weren't paying attention to before. I will forever pay attention to these things because I am thankful I can hear them:

1. When you run your hand across a chair arm, it makes a noise

2. She heard something whispered to another person when she wasn't looking straight at them

3. Before, some kids would find it hilarious to walk up to my girl and mouth words with their mouth but not really say anything. Since we have now discovered she was reading lips all this time, she would say "Wait, what did you say?" to the kids. Then they would leave laughing at her response basically making fun of her. When this happened for the first time after she got her "little miracles"(her hearing aids) she shouted and pointed her finger at them and said "HA! You

weren't saying anything!"   TAKE THAT mean
kids!

4. When the heat cut on in the house she was a
bit frightened having never heard that before

5. When the ice maker dropped ice it scared her
to death. On her first day to school with little
miracles, the pencil sharpener scared her to death

6. Now she responds immediately when spoken
to

7. Her eyes are bright

8. She is extremely happy and laughs a lot

9. She makes noises with her mouth and laughs

10. She talks in all kinds of funny voices and
laughs at her sounds

11. She taps her fingers just to hear the sound

12. She "gets" jokes and sarcasm that she never did before because she couldn't hear it

13. She hates having to take her hearing aids out at night because she says she can't hear anything and she goes back to a dark world she lived in before and she doesn't like that world anymore

14. She said she feels like she is "normal" with her little miracles in

15. When she went to school she was bouncing around telling and showing everyone about her little miracles and one kid said, "Aren't you embarrassed that you have hearing aids?" My girl replied, "NO! Because I can HEAR!"

16. Before we arrived at the audiologists office, my girl was worried about what the hearing aids would look like, would she look like an old woman, etc. Once they were programmed and placed in her ears, that was no longer a

discussion. She quickly realized that what they look like did not matter because it was so great to hear

17. She says, "I hear that!" a lot.

18. She was at her babysitting job that she does regularly, and she told the little doll to stop smacking her mouth when she was eating. The little doll said, "But I always eat like this and you never said anything before". My girl said, "Well if I have ever heard your smacking I would have told you a long time ago to stop smacking, so stop smacking please."

19. She said the Pledge of Allegiance for the first time. She knew it, but never knew where they were in it, so didn't participate. Said it sounded like Charlie Brown's teacher before.

20. Coming out of church she said she had heard the most beautiful singing. She knew I always

said she had a beautiful voice but she never heard it.

21. She has stopped smacking her mouth when she eats even though we have told her to stop for years, but she didn't understand why we told her that because she couldn't hear it. Now she will smack loudly on purpose and laugh about it

Before I tell my favorite story of them all, I will say that my girl has given me permission to share this. It is the most precious moment we have had, it is hilarious, but precious coming from an 17 year old girl, almost 18. At first she thought it was too embarrassing to tell, but I told her what the moral of the story is, and she wanted me to share it. So read carefully and enjoy, but don't forget the moral at the end. Enjoy:

We were leaving the audiologists office with her newfound freedom into the world of hearing. Driving home, she had called my mom to tell her she could hear. In the middle of the conversation, she threw the phone down and started laughing hysterically, rocking back and forth with tears streaming down her face from hard laughing. This went on for minutes. She was laughing so hard she couldn't speak. I said, "What is going on?" She said, "Mom! I just farted and it made the funniest sound I have ever heard!" Then she proceeded to laugh uncontrollably along with me.

Folks, the moral of that story is this: May we never again hear the sound of an annoying fart that will stink up the joint without laughing uncontrollably, for we were able to hear the sound. We have become so immune to the sound that we get exasperated with the scent. May we all live our lives appreciating how funny a fart sounds from this day forward. Amen.

My Inner Fat Chick

I have a dose of my reality for you. I share these things because I want you to know you are not alone.

Yesterday I was in Walmart looking at summer clothes and they had rearranged some things so that the plus sized clothes were where the workout clothes used to be. I didn't realize it and picked up an adorable shirt only to discover it was plus sized. I have worn plus sized clothes many times in my life. I actually thought to myself, "I could eat what I want and wear this and it's cute." My inner fat chick was coming out. I quickly had to shove her back under the covers and smother her. It is sickening to me to think that this is my day to day reality - to shove a fat mentality down on a daily basis. Shouldn't I be home free once I figure out to eat less and move more?? I guess not. Every moment I have to make up my mind that I am going to eat less and move more. When I have a bad moment and eat something I shouldn't or eat too much then I immediately start over and regroup and say to myself "I'm starting again now".

Suppressing my inner fat chick is incredibly frustrating especially when you feel like you do the right things and still gain weight or are still wanting something you shouldn't have. Distraction or drinking water, well, that works if you have will power to do them. Most times I do, but sometimes I don't and I cave.

One of the things I do to keep myself from eating things is I ask myself, "Is this worth the calories?" Most of the time it is not. So many things we eat are not even all that good. But we are eating them anyway to fulfill some need we have whether it is comfort or emotion or perceived hunger or we are in a social situation and everyone else is eating so we feel we should too. So ask yourself, "Is this worth the calories?" If the answer is no then shove the inner fat chick or dude and smother her or him.

My other technique is different. If I decide to eat something I shouldn't then I say to myself "Now you have to run three miles to work that off, is it worth it?" Sometimes it is worth it and I get out there and run to work it off. Other times I refuse to eat the dessert because I don't want to do the work to maintain my weight.

Here's the deal: EVERY DAY IS A STRUGGLE. I keep up with my weight so that it won't creep back on me and one fine day I wake up overweight again. If I'm a pound or two heavy one day then I make adjustments in my eating that day and hope tomorrow will be a better weigh day. I used to be anti scale. I bought a scale so weight won't creep back. Now, I have an idea every day how my day needs to be. Now if you are trying to lose weight, stay off the scale! But if you are trying to maintain, I have found it to be a good tool. If you are trying to lose weight then the scale, I have found, will be a problem in that you will give up more easily if you don't see results you want. Muscle does weigh more than fat. As you get more active you will build muscle so the scale is not your friend to lose. The scale is a friend to maintain. Scale or no scale, plus size or petite, tall or short,

167

you are enough. I am enough. In a world of too much, you are enough, regardless of how much you weigh.

Being Authentic Part 2

Being authentic involves realizing you are not perfect and neither is anyone else no matter what kind of persona they like to present. It is incredibly freeing to admit and advertise your lack of perfection. I like to put an amusing spin on things that happen. After all, if we don't laugh about life then we would all sit around crying. I choose to laugh. Your attitude is key to living an authentic life. You will feel trapped if you try to keep putting on an air of perfection.

I love a picture that one of my friends posted on social media. It was a picture of their mound of laundry that needed to be folded captioned as "Art Deco Laundry Sculpture". Folks, that would be a real example of living an authentic life. All of us have a mound of laundry just like my friend, but I pillow my head tonight knowing I am not alone in the struggle to keep up with washing and folding. So many don't feel free to post everyday life. It keeps it real, makes others feel a sense of commonality, and helps us realize we are not alone. We are not alone with laundry or with life.

For years I have mentioned that I lost the Mother of the Year contest. One day I may be a winner for serving donuts for dinner, another day I may loose for forgetting I told my daughter I would come eat lunch at school with her. The fact is that the illustrious status of Mother of the Year is a tedious honor that walks a very thin rope. One minute you are a shoe in for saving the science project from certain doom when your son's volcano erupts and the lava is melting the paint but you swoop in with your mother of the year cape and save the day by helping touch up the paint. The next minute you are out because you forgot today was 4-h and you didn't make muffins with your daughter. Own it. The fact of the matter is that we all are Mother of the Year in our child's eyes. Even though we fail and succeed on a daily basis. You are enough for your children. I am enough for mine.

Admitting you aren't perfect is like releasing the valve on a pressure cooker. It's just too much effort to try to be perfect. Embrace your imperfection and share it with other imperfect people. Putting an amusing spin on everyday life is just like smiling: it's contagious. Let's create an epidemic and find our authentic selves.

Uniquely Genius

When your children are born, no one expects to sit across a table and have someone say to them, "Your child has Autism". No one wants to hear "Your child would benefit from services provided in the special education program." No one wants to hear, "We have eliminated all other possibilities and your child meets enough criteria to be diagnosed with Attention Deficit Disorder."

I have a degree in Elementary Education. I have had the college level classes on all of these diagnosis. I have sat at a table when I have had to tell a parent each one of these phrases as an educator. But let me tell you this: NOTHING that I learned in college, or as a teacher prepared me to hear these words about my own child. After all, my children are perfect in my eyes. I thought I would birth the straight A student, the honor roll kid, the valedictorian, the quarterback of the football team, the star soccer player, the softball player with the full ride scholarship kid. Didn't you think you would birth these children? I was taught so much more by my children about what "perfect" really is. For this, I am grateful.

Two different times, in the second grade and again in the sixth grade I was told that my child should be held back. I knew that it would damage their self esteem and that their academics would be in no better condition by repeating as opposed to being moved to the next grade with their friends. It was a gut feeling, but in the end, my gut was right. Had I allowed them to hold my child back, they

173

may very well have ended up dropping out of school or had such low self image that they would have never recovered. The fact is that the school was judging my child's ability to climb a tree when my child was actually good at swimming. Had I played into the school's hand of cards, the outcome would have been so different from what it is. My child was diagnosed with a language processing learning disability in which we were told they could not get what was processed in their head to write it down on a piece of paper. In the meantime my child was labeled "stupid", or "special ed", or "dumb blonde". So many times over the years I wanted to bang my fist on the table and ask if they noticed how intelligent my child was, or how great a Christian young person my child was, or what a great friend to others my child was? All the while we judge others on the world's scale when we need to be judging on God's scale and accepting everyone and their rainbow of differences. Instead, it seems that we judge everyone based on the world's scale and expect all the fish and the squirrels to climb the tree exactly the same, as Albert Einstein so eloquently quoted.

We all need to realize that no one is dumb. We all are varying degrees of smart. After all, God made us all perfectly the way He wanted us to be. Autistic, Learning Disabled, Attention Deficit Disorder, Hyperactivity: these are all labels created by man to describe people who don't seem to be able to climb trees like the squirrels can. Indeed, we should put the squirrels in the pool and see how well they can swim. I am enough. You are enough. Our children are enough. In a world of too much, we are enough.

175

No Score

There are a lot of things that a score is important. A baseball game is insignificant if there is no score. A tennis match is the same. A football game would not be as exciting without a posted score as would a hockey game. Some even comment that they need to "even" the score with a positive OR negative connotation. Today I would like to suggest that there is one aspect of life where there should be no score.

I suppose this is a pet peeve of mine. I do something for someone and they say, "I owe you one." Heaven help us if when someone does something for me they think in their head "She owes me one" because let me clue

you in on something about me, it ain't happening. I don't think to myself "_____ did something for me now I have to even the score and I have to do something for them."
It takes the joy from the giver if the giver feels like you feel obligated to even the score and return a favor. In turn, it takes the joy out of receiving something if you feel guilty and immediately in your head think that you need to repay them.

The Bible talks about God loving a cheerful giver. I am suggesting that if you expect something in return for your giving, whether it be giving of time, talent, or money, then you are not ultimately a cheerful giver. Give with the intention of making someone happy or their life easier without expecting anything in return. If you are expecting something in return or the score to be evened at some point, then you are taking the joy away from the recipient. The recipient should be able to accept without worry that you are expecting something in return.

On the same token, if you are the recipient, be a gracious recipient without feeling obligated to return the favor. If you feel a sense of obligation then you are taking the joy away from the giver. They gave to you to make your life easier or to make you happy. Be happy and skip the guilt. Guilt is a terrible thing. It can rule your life. It can undermine your efforts.

I am a fan of paying it forward. After all, what goes around always comes around and you reap what you sow. So if we all are paying it forward then we all experience the joy of giving and receiving without the mental anguish of obligation and guilt. It makes my head hurt to think of all the people I would "owe" for helping me or my family. Let's just do what we can, when we can to who we can and we will all be reaping the harvest of good people doing good things in a good world.

Breakfast on the Porch-A Dog's Story

I have had pets. I had a cat named Muffin growing up. I loved that cat. I dressed her up and she took whatever I dished out to her. She was my friend. I would shudder to count the number of pets we have had since we married 28 years ago. It is probably in the 30's. They have come and gone for one reason or another. They were all bubble pets meaning they were on the bubble pending pottying on the carpet and then they were out! We got a dog for the Boy. He was a good dog, a bulging, beastly dog that protected my boy and served his duty well. He kept the boy from being scared in the house. Where the boy went, the dog followed. I guess I loved that dog, but not for myself, I loved that dog for who he was to my boy.   And then there was Zoe.

Once our boy's dog died and our last cat passed on, I said "No More". In my deepest thoughts I was thrilled to be done with the mess of animals. Then one fine day my oldest decided she wanted to get a dog. About to go to college, I said, "Oh NO!" We ended up making a deal. If she would stay away from a toxic situation she had involved herself in then she could have the dog. It was worth a dog if she would stay out of a bad situation. Well, she held up to her end of the bargain and she picked out a dog from a breeder. I thought this had disaster written all over it. I was gunna be caring for a dog and she was going to graduate and leave for college. What in the world? SHE picked out the dog, SHE paid for the dog, SHE called and checked out the breeder, SHE did all the legwork. I was totally not involved and not interested. Amen.

Well, she was cute.

But whatever, I was not involved.

Then she came home and I was determined to teach her to potty train. She was really cute. And cuddly. And sweet. But whatever, I was not involved.

She was really sweet though.

Which brings me to my story today: I love the dog even though I fought so hard not to. I don't know what I ever did without her. I dress her up, play with her, hold her, feed her a bottle. It's crazy really. I never thought I could care for an animal like I do this one. So this morning I was about to feed her breakfast which consists of a fourth of a peanut butter sandwich on wheat bread with a half teaspoon of Angel Eyes(which keeps her face white). She won't eat the Angel Eyes any other way. And that is A-ok because, well, she is my baby. So I sit down on the couch, where I usually do, to pinch the sandwich and feed it to her, and she won't come over to me. She keeps twisting her head and body toward the door. I think, well, we have a revelation and the dog needs to go potty. So I take her out and she stands on the porch then sits on the porch. She proceeds to look up at me. I said, "Did you want your breakfast on the porch this morning?" She jumped up and down and I sat down on the porch and fed her breakfast to her. Breakfast on the porch. Alrighty then.

Every animal deserves to be loved like my Zoe. She found me. She adopted me. Thank you, my oldest, for the gift of Zoe, for she

183

brings me great joy every day. I am involved. I love her.

Addendum to this story: At almost exactly one year old, Zoe was hit by a car. I was devastated. My oldest daughter may have picked out and bought the dog, but animals have a crazy way of adopting their human. I was Zoe's human. I have had other dogs since Zoe but none adopted me like she did. I sincerely hope that one day there will be another Zoe for me. Not a Zoe to replace Zoe, but another Zoe who has my heart like she did. She is in a beautiful garden in my backyard still today and I still, unbeknownst to my family, go visit her regularly. Zoe was the one animal in my life that made me feel like I was enough. Just by being herself, Zoe needed me and I was enough for her. I was enough. You are enough. In a world of too much, you are enough.

No Reading for Me-A Story of Prom Hair

We made an appointment for my oldest to get her prom hair and makeup done at the local beauty school. Upon checking around, the average price for just fixing hair for an event, not even cutting it, is around $80. We are folks on a budget so this was not going to work thus we chose the local beauty school. Reasonably priced, and no cutting to be done, we felt confident in this decision.

The school told us the appointment would take 2 hours so I packed my iPad so I could read while she was getting her hair and makeup done. I also brought my camera to capture these moments on film.

We arrived and waited for our hairdresser. Time passed and our hairdresser was still busy with her previous head of hair. Being at the beauty school I began to pray for whoever was still in that chair for fear the color went awry or the cut was bad. Soon, they called us back and said, "She still isn't done so we are going to let you go ahead and get started with this girl." I am from the South and a firm believer that you can say what you want to as long as you include "Bless her/his heart". The girl that was to fix my girl's prom hair had voluntarily made herself the ugliest hairdo I had ever laid eyes on bless her heart. She had shaved half her head and the rest of it she had sewn hair into and you could see where the hair had been sewn into it. It was a sight to behold. I recognized right then that I was not going to get any reading done here today lest my daughter end up with some experiment in terror that the poor hairdresser defined as an updo. And so it began...

187

My daughter showed the picture of the hair that she wanted and it was confirmed that it could, indeed, be done. She then proceeded to get the can of hairspray announcing that they keep that kind in stock just for her because she singlehandedly goes through cans in a day. Oh my.

Still holding out hope that some reading may be had during this time, the updo was started with the part. She parted my daughters hair just over her ear somewhat in the flavor of a bad combover. I said, "Oh no no no, we want to go with her natural part up here" and proceeded to show where we wanted the part to be. I also proceeded to put up my iPad resigning myself to the fact that not a word would be read today. Amen.

The teasing commenced, the hairspray blew, the announcement was made that "I don't believe in bobby pins, I just use hairspray, this hair ain't goin nowhere". Indeed it isn't. Now her hair actually was looking fabulous even though there was not a bobby pin 1 in her head and an F5 tornado was not going to move a strand of the hair. It became comical. If you tried to pick up a strand, the entire head of hair would lift up. She looked gorgeous!! Even though you could have thrown a brick at her head and it would not have damaged her skull. She even did a prom jumping picture and her hair stayed totally in place :)

On to makeup, our bless her heart girl was good at makeup. But we didn't escape hairspray. She was spraying my daughter's face with hairspray to set the makeup. What in

189

the world? Again, when it was finished, she looked gorgeous!

Our experience at the beauty school was just fine. We got the outcome we desired in spite of the appearance of the gal who did the work. But, I never did get a single word read while I was there...you just can't read while a bless her heart girl works on your girl's hair for fear that in one blink of the eye your daughter may end up half bald or with a part reminiscent of a bad combover. So the moral of the story is: Keep both eyes open when you get an updo at the beauty school!

Enjoying the Silence, and Practicing Being Still

I grew up as an only child. I wanted more than one child so they had brothers and sisters around. Not because I didn't enjoy silence growing up myself but because I revel in noise. I enjoy organized chaos. I am a master of multitasking. I was the child who could listen in class to everything the teacher said while I was listening to music, reading a book, looking at a magazine, and checking out the new hairdo of the person sitting in front of me. But if you asked me a question, I could tell you in detail everything that was said or done in that class that day. I am a perfect to be the mom of more than one child. God blessed me with three.

He also made me a kindergarten teacher. I revel in that organized chaos also. I can paint handprints, listen to a story of how your dog pooped on your carpet and your mom cleaned it up, acknowledge that one needs to go to the restroom, sharpen a pencil, write down a phone number, and keep paint off of a boutique outfit all at the same time without losing my mind. I like noise. I always have. I am not a quiet person. I recently found out I am hard of hearing in my left ear. I am not surprised because I am such a loud person there must have been a reason. Now I know why. I had to be loud enough to overcome hearing loss.

I have been doing an experiment in silence by turning the television off. I have not voluntarily turned it on in years. The Bible says "Be still and know that I am God." I wonder sometimes how often I take time to be still and know that He is God. In all the noise I get lost sometimes and fail to hear God. So I turned some of the noise off. There is nothing worth watching on it anyway. I have not missed it one bit. I have been able to hear so many other things that I would not have heard otherwise. Sometimes the tv is on just for background noise. What in the world? Why do we need background noise? To drown out our lives? Are we that miserable? I, for one, am not. I do not need background noise to fill my life. I want to fill my life with important things.

I ran a race in Atlanta a few months ago. A total stranger came up to me and said, "I like your hair!" I said, "Thanks!" After a pause she came back to me again and said, "Do you run with it like that?" I wanted to say, No, I put it in a ponytail when I run. But I didn't give that remark. I politely said, "Yes I do. It is a very heat, humidity, and wind resistant hairdo for me." This conversation left me scratching my head and got me to thinking.

It occurred to me that people are uncomfortable with silence. We feel the need to fill the air with words. The lady couldn't be content to end the conversation with she liked my hair and that be enough. Because we were still standing there, she continued talking and ended up saying something that was a bit silly. Why are we so uncomfortable with silence?

I challenge us all to take time to crave silence. Take time to enjoy silence. Take time to sit in a room and actually talk to our family without a television on to engage us. It is very freeing. Take out the background noise from your life. We don't need it. All it does is clutter our lives with useless conversation that takes away from interaction with people who are important. Be still. We are enough without the extra noise. I am enough. You are enough. In a world of too much, we are enough.

One Day at a Time-A How To

There are three parts to life: past, present and future. The past is gone. We can't do anything about it, we can't change it, we can't get it back, we can't redo it. If we are baptized believers living a faithful life then our future is secure. The tomorrow that we look forward to NEVER comes. Think about it. When "tomorrow" gets here it is "today".

The reason God only gives us this moment is because he knows that if we were aware of the details of our future, we would be engulfed. If we could do something with our past, we would be submerged in murky undergrowth. God created us and He knew that we could only handle this very second in time. Thus, that is what He gave us. And yet we try to juggle everything else too.

When you become overwhelmed, think on these things: The past is gone, we can't do anything about it. Our future is secure, it is guaranteed. All we need to focus on is what is right here right now. God gave us today to sort through because it is all we could manage. We are the ones that take on too much thought and overwhelm ourselves the deluge of emotions, history and future possibilities. God wants us to focus our energy on what is in front of us right now.. The past is gone, He has secured our future.

What a wonderful feeling of peace to know that I only have to handle my today. Today is enough.

Barefoot Running-A New Endeavor and Consumer Report

I remember when I was about 11, I heard the melodious sound of the ice cream man on the streets behind where I grew up. Living on the main road, the ice cream man did not go down my street so I had to go behind the house and through the neighbor's yards to get to him. Most times I did not catch him because it was too much trouble and my mother was so good about keeping plenty of treats in our freezer. This day I decided to chase down that man who brings zombie eyes to any child who hears his tune in the area.

What is it about the ice cream man's music? It is ages old and children have reacted to it the same way for a century if he has been around that long. I was barefooted in the backyard when I heard his music and ran to stick my head in the door to shout that I was chasing the ice cream man and off I went. I still remember how free I felt running like a crazy child chasing after the sound of music to buy a refreshment.

I never have had much use for shoes. I love being barefoot. You will be hard pressed to find me with shoes on from April to October unless I am somewhere that requires them. My feet are tough and I can even walk in gravel and aggregate with no shoes. I started running years ago and of course, run in shoes. Then I read this book called <u>Born to Run</u> about American Indians running barefoot or in sandals. Our bodies are designed to run and all the padding of running shoes are just man's creation when we were all born to run.

The birth of my desire to run barefooted came from that book. Luckily, barefoot running was becoming a fad so there were many choices to "transition" from shoes to bare feet. However, being on a budget and already having running shoes it was hard for me to decide that I would spend more money on minimalist shoes or 5 finger shoes. My philosophy in life is go big or go home so I just decided, after a LOT of research, that I would just run completely barefooted. I LOVED it. I ran about a half a mile barefooted after a 4 mile run in my shoes. My feet were very sore and I was really nervous about hitting a rock or something that would cut my foot open. I have children to raise so I am always concerned about my safety and injuring myself. Also through research I realized that I would be starting over when I started running barefoot so the fact that I was training for a half marathon seemed not the smartest time to start barefoot running. Idea axed, shoes back on, thought moved to the back of my head.

But...I never gave up the desire to barefoot run. Every pair of shoes I buy I think to myself, "I have to buy the least padded, hardest soled running shoe in the store or my legs get sore from too much padding. So WHY do I buy shoes to run in??" And eternally, I look at the Vibram 5 finger shoes. Then I look away because I am afraid to waste my money on something I may not like or be able to use and wouldn't they rub blisters between your toes?

I was at the tent sale at Sports Seasons. Vibram 5 Fingers were on sale plus an extra 20% off. Sold to the rock star with spiky hair.

I skipped away like the leper who had been dipped in the River Jordan! So excited!

I took those puppies out for a spin on a Monday for the first time. I was super pumped. I decided I would start with walking some then run until I was uncomfortable. I thought that was a solid plan for breaking them in. I never got uncomfortable, my toes never rubbed, I just felt free as a bird like I was chasing the ice cream man and was LOVING it! These shoes are as close to barefoot as possible without actually having your skin on the pavement. So it eased my fears of stepping on something and cutting my foot open. They seriously feel like I am totally barefoot.

I would recommend the five finger shoes for running if a consumer generally likes to go barefoot for normal activity or out in the yard, has moderately tough feet, and wears stability shoes which generally have firm padding in them.

They are very comfortable, I found there to be no break in time needed as I was able to run almost 5 miles with no problems the very first time I put them on my feet. I am unusual with the "no break in" time needed. Most people have to start with very minimal mileage and work up. I have not experienced that. They do have 5 finger toe socks to wear with them but I wore them barefooted.

I am going to be a complete convert to 5 Finger shoes. I want to wear them all the time. Best.Shoes.Ever. These shoes allowed me to be my authentic self.   Being an individual who loves being barefooted, my feet were enough for these shoes.

I Just Want to Drive a Bus

I spent a lot of my younger adult life teaching Bible class and not enjoying it, borderline despising it which is somewhat surprising since I am a teacher by profession. After years of guilt for not enjoying the experience, I realized that there was more to do in the church for the womenfolk than just teaching Bible class. I decided I wanted to drive the bus. I didn't know at the time the magnitude of what God had in mind for me in my "transportation ministry" but it sure has been exciting so far. This is the story of how my commercial drivers license actually came into being.

The idea of driving the church bus seemed simple enough in theory and I was super excited to get started with achieving my goal. I went to the DMV to get my handy dandy booklet to study for the written test. Upon picking up the "booklet" I was aghast at the practically college textbook size of the manual. Oh well, a little study never hurt anyone. I took the manual home and got to work. My goal was to go take the test in two weeks.

I cracked open the manual to pages and pages of diagrams of engines, semi trucks, hazardous chemical labels to memorize, and various other "junk" they expected me to know to drive the church bus. Did they realize I just want to drive the church bus? In all reality I had never really checked under the hood of anything. Doesn't Jiffy Lube do that?

I guess I will learn if I want to drive the church bus...

I studied HARD for that two weeks. I had to read over and over the same stuff to open my head and pour in the knowledge. My head hurt the whole second week. Literally. Good thing I have enough determination to share with the free world or I would have thrown in the towel when I saw the manual.

I went to the DMV to take the test. It was on the computer and multiple choice. I am convinced it is a conspiracy with the wording of the questions. I failed the test.

Just like that, I was back to the drawing board. They won't let you take the test again for 2 weeks. So, in 14 days, I was back to sit in line and take it again after another 336 hours of learning about coupling devices and axels. Failed a second time.

The third time I went to take the test I was just about mad. Don't these people realize that I am not going to drive a tractor trailer truck for BP hauling hazardous chemicals? I JUST want to drive the church bus. Unfortunately you have to be able to know how to haul hazardous chemicals in order to drive a church bus... Well, in the middle of my test, my phone rang and I saw on caller ID that it was the room mother for my youngest daughters class so I answered it. She needed me to bring cupcakes for the Halloween party. I got a tap on the shoulder and a not so nice voice said, "You are dismissed from the testing area for answering your phone. That is cheating." What? Do I even KNOW anyone who could answer your crazy computer questions? I was in tears explaining the call was about cupcakes. Long story short, I couldn't come back for a month because I was cheating.

You can't keep a good girl down so in a month I was back! And I passed!! Now I could move on to learning to drive!

I solicited the help of a gentleman at church who had experience with the bus. He showed me how to parallel park and how to dock park and alley load. Not that I would be doing any of that, but I had to know it for the driving test. I got out on the road and practiced a lot. When I went for the driving test I had to also do a pre-trip inspection of the bus including getting under the bus and checking certain points to make sure the bus is safe for driving.

I had to have another CDL driver with me to take me to the testing site for the drivers test. The same gentleman took me. The man who did my test was what you would expect, rough and brash. He asked me to point out what I need to check before I drive. There were 75 points I had to orally state with no help from a paper or checklist. I got all 75 without missing a beat.

The man asked me what I was going to do when I break down with a bus load of people. I said, "sir, I just want to drive the church bus so I am going to call the church and say, I've got a bus load of blue hairs and we are broke down on the side of the road so send someone to get us." Then I politely preceded with what he wanted me to tell him which was how to fire a flare and where to place my triangle hazards.

The evaluator and I got into the bus and went on with the actual driving part including the parallel parking and alley dock. I did all of that without a single mistake. The man was very complimentary of my skills. I resisted the urge to tell him all I had been through to get to this point. I kindly went inside and smiled for my picture and got my commercial drivers license.

I can finally drive the bus!! Now if you want to ride my bus with a car battery in tow, I'm not letting you on because it is dangerous. I know this because I studied. And since I know there will be many who try to get on my bus with a car battery in their arms I am prepared to not let them on. I also know that I need to put a strap every 10 feet on my trailer if I am hauling uncovered items with my semi. These are other things that will be

211

useful to me I just know it. I can also dismantle and assemble coupling devices to attach my trailer to my semi since I use that all the time too.

The lesson in all of this is to be determined. Dream big and go for it! Never be too old to learn something new. Be your authentic self. You are enough, just the way you are.

Crypt Flies, Tissue Vendors, and Funeral Home Follies

When your husband works in the funeral industry people are just dying to know the ins and outs of such a job. Luckily, I am here to educate you on these things. Tonight you will be able to sleep well because some of your strangest questions will now have an answer.

I am always excited to be invited to my husband's events. I would be able to attend more of them if we didn't have children at home that want to be fed. I thought I fed them yesterday but they are wanting to eat again. Anyway, yesterday I was able to go to the Funeral Directors Convention as arm candy for my husband. I try to play my role well and clean up real nice. Last night was no exception. However, for a middle aged woman who is expected to play the role of the "life of the party," a late night event will be full of yawns and wonderings of just when I will get to bed. To remedy this I decided to take an evening nap so I would be fresh for the gathering. I dozed off around 5:30 and woke up right at 8:30 which was the time I was told to meet my husband at the party. I jumped up, freshened up my makeup, zipped my little black dress then noticed I had sheet marks on my arms. Apparently I had a really nice nap. As luck would have it, I had thrown a black sweater in my truck so was able to wear that to cover the sheet marks on my arms. Ready, set, GO! I am off to play the role of arm candy which I LOVE to play. I got downstairs to the lobby of the hotel where the convention is being held and took my position on the arm of the most handsome man I know and begin to socialize with the Funeral

Directors. 10 minutes into the social hour, my husband leans over to me and says, "You have sheet marks on your face." I reply with, " I had a really good nap apparently. I will keep my head turned this way until the sheet marks subside."

Contrary to what you might think, being around funeral directors is very fun and entertaining. I love it actually. They are a jovial bunch. The persona you see when you are at need in their facility is a 360 compared to how they are in real life. I guess they are around so much sadness at work that they really ham it up around each other in social settings. One musing I heard was a group laughing about a horrible incident where a body kept leaking through the mouth and they had to keep wiping the body's mouth hoping the family would not notice. Another was a

215

director talking about a mouth not being stitched tight enough and it came open during the night and the subsequent scrambling to get the mouth sewn back shut before the family arrived and saw the situation.

Being a funeral director and embalmer is actually artistry. They take their work seriously and want to please the family to have a good remembrance of their loved one. However, as with any job, there are times when things just happen. Like crypt flies. Did you know there was such a thing as crypt flies? They only breed in dead bodies. They resemble gnats. Funeral homes can buy a "crypt fly bug zapper" which resembles an air conditioner. So the next time you are at a funeral home look around for an air conditioner type thing. It may not really be an air conditioner but a crypt fly zapper that keeps the pesky pests under control.

Also available for purchase is a computer program that will prevent you from accidentally digging up another body while making a spot for a new arrival. It's a pricy piece of software but I can see the need there. I would hate to disturb Aunt Edna while making room for Uncle George. This piece of equipment is extremely useful when you own an older cemetery where some markers may be so old and unreadable and possibly dislodged. This piece will get you back in line without dislodging a decayed relative.

My favorite quote of the night was from a funeral home owner talking amongst the group we were sitting with. He said, "I have GOT to get my sales up." I just scratched my head thinking how he could do that aside from going out and murdering a few or digging a hole and leading a herd of folks out on a senior citizens event where they accidentally fall into the hole. Seriously, how would he increase his sales? He also stated that he doesn't sell many markers since he is 80% cremation. These are all normal conversations amongst funeral directors. Now these Funeral Directors are being their authentic selves. They are enough and so are you.

Be Flawesome

I was at a festival a while back, minding my own business and shopping with my daughter. From out of nowhere, I heard a strange voice say "I need you to model my clothes for me. I can tell you are just the person I need." When I realized she was talking to me, I was dumbfounded. I told her I would be happy to model her clothes for her. She said, "I can't find a single person anywhere who has the confidence to let me take their picture for my website." I was more than willing to help the lady out but the whole experience has left me still scratching my head today. Are we really at a point in our lives that we feel so meek about ourselves that this poor woman could not find a single person to model her clothes that was willing to have their picture made? I think it is deplorable to see the breakdown of self worth. I have enough self esteem to share with the free world, and I realize that is a bit unusual. It bothers me that more people don't hold themselves in high esteem. It's no wonder that families are failing and marriages are failing because you can't love others if you don't love yourself.

We all have flaws. My belly is my problem area. Others have problems with their legs, or hips or ears or whatever. Truth is, we are all made in God's image and there is no ugly involved in God's image. So we are all beautiful. A good personality trumps physical beauty any day of the week. If you don't have a good personality then it's just "congratulations on your face". It's what is on the inside that matters. I have a friend who is super petite and little and cute. One time,

220

she was going to a formal event and was having the worst trouble finding a dress to wear. She said that the formal department did not have anything that was little enough for her and the children's department did not have anything old enough looking for her. It was then that I embraced my belly and realized that EVERYONE has trouble finding clothes to look good no matter your size or shape. Everyone struggles. So stop looking at other people and thinking how much better looking they are than you are. Just stop. Mommas, don't be saying negative things about yourself in front of your children. They are watching and we need to raise a new generation of good, positive self imaged youngsters.

I went a few weeks ago for my federal department of transportation physical and the doctor told me that I was morbidly obese.

WHAT? I told him it was a good thing I had good self esteem because some women would starve themselves over a statement like that. I also told him a few other things to put him in his place. And then I sat on him. I also said to the receptionist when I exited(loud enough for the doctor to hear me) "Get a good look at me because you are looking at the face of the morbidly obese." I feel like I got my point across to everyone in that doctors office. It's a wonder he didn't write that I wasn't able to renew my commercial drivers license because I am so heavy I would pop a bus tire.

I have clothes in my closet right now that are sized from 12-18 and ALL of them fit. If the number on the tag of your clothes bothers you, then cut the tag out. You don't need that kind of negativity in your life. Buy clothes that fit. Some of these clothes are made in

China and they are made to fit small people who can wad themselves up and sleep in drawers like it was a bed. These numbers are unrealistic. Try on clothes and buy ones that fit no matter what the tag says. When we have clothes on that fit, our confidence level goes up. If we are refusing to buy a bigger size clothes then we are just making ourselves miserable. Embrace your body for what it is and move forward. Put on the swimsuit. Buy a bigger size. Eat the pie. None of us are getting out of here alive so enjoy life and accept yourself for the shape that you are. Everything in moderation. As we age, it becomes harder and harder to lose weight. Don't define yourself by your ability to keep a pristine figure. Fluffy people give better hugs. Exercise, eat in moderation, buy clothes that fit, and PLEASE decide each morning that your will love yourself. We all are a hot mess. Some just hide it better than others. We are all flawed. Get out there and flaunt your awesome every single day. Be FLAWESOME!!

The Secret to Life

I'm about to reveal to you the secret to life. This was life changing for me. Did you know that we don't have to have everything figured out? When situations present themselves to us and we don't know which way to turn or what to do with the situation, we don't have to have a plan? Did you know that? I didn't. But when I figured it out years ago, my life changed. Dramatically.

You see, when we become overwhelmed with life and with children and jobs and family and friends and stuff and holidays and problems and relationships and cleaning the house and...the list goes on and becomes staggering if you think about all of it at once to figure it out. We don't have to sort through every detail. All we have to do is the next right thing. Whatever that is.

Some days the next right thing may be to stop at Sonic and get a half price drink. Some days doing the next right thing may be going to get your teeth cleaned. Some days it could be to simply take a nap. Sometimes the next right thing could be making a phone call to someone who has hurt you. In some instances, the next right thing is a major step and in of circumstances it is a small thing like giving someone a hug.

I've always been taught not to pick up hitchhikers. I have never picked up a stranger off the street because I was taught not to. Every day when I leave for work there are two guys I see come out of the house just outside my subdivision. They walk to work which happens to be the Mexican restaurant close to my house. Every time I see these guys I wanted to pick them up and take them to work. It's not that far out of the way. I struggled with this desire for over a year. The voice inside my head kept telling me no, you don't pick up strangers. One day, it was 19 degrees outside when I left for work. I saw the guys walking down the street. I stopped. I couldn't watch them walk in this weather. So I did the next right thing which was to stop and roll my window down. I spoke to them and realized they didn't speak English. Best I could, I communicated that I would take them to their work. They got in and smiled so big I can't even describe it. We tried to talk but I didn't speak Spanish and they didn't speak English. But when I dropped them off at their work, their gratitude transcended any language barriers. Kindness knows no language and the next right thing is all I had to do. Now I pick them up every day and we enjoy our ride to work together. You see, I didn't have to replay every terrible scenario that could happen from picking up strangers. All I had to do was the next right thing. And that day, it was stop and roll my window down. Rolling my window down led to one of the highlights of my day every day.

That is just one of the examples I can give of being blessed by doing the next right thing. Don't try to figure it all out, just do what's next. One step. One thing. One decision. One gut feeling. That's all. With this secret to life, I have gained a sense of peace and joy in my life. I hope this helps you too.

Just do the next right thing. Whatever that is. It may be turning out the light and going back to sleep. Martin Luther King said that Faith is taking the first step without seeing the whole staircase. Jennifer says do the next right thing. Same concept, different perspective.

Storage

I noticed that a gorgeous piece of undeveloped property close to where I live is now being built upon. What are they building is a valid question and the answer to that is a storage facility. A place with rows and rows of storage garages of various sizes to rent for your excess stuff. I think these places are great for people who are in transition of some type who need a place to store things until they are settled somewhere else. A family with a boat may need that to store their watercraft, car or recreational vehicle that won't fit on the property at home. For those people, there is a storage facility just around the corner from the one that is now being built. Two storage facilities built within two miles of each other.

There are shows on television about people who go to storage facilities and buy the garage contents sight unseen hoping there is something valuable in the unit. The storage owners are actually having to auction the contents of storage units that have outstanding rent, abandoned units, etc. WHAT are we storing that we can't keep at home?? Are we at a point in life where we keep so much "stuff" that we can't even keep it all in our home and we even forget about what is in the unit? Are we buying so much junk that we don't really need that we end up with an overage that warrants an extra monthly payment to store it all?

WHAT are we doing? This all occurred to me as I noticed this new storage area being built. Clearly there is need for two storage facilities two miles apart or they would not be building it. We have THAT much junk to warrant such building. Bless.

In a world of overindulgence, I long for simplicity, crave less, am satisfied more, and am blessed more than I deserve. The more stuff you accumulate, the more stuff floats around in your head producing anxiety, stress, breakdowns, and a sense of general unhappiness. We have so much that we need a storage unit for the excess and we can't even remember most of what is in the unit. Enough excess that a show has been made to chronicle the auctions and what is found in abandoned storage units. I pray that my storage unit is full of peace, happiness, contented feelings, love, joy, patience, kindness, goodness, faithfulness, gentleness, self control, and good works. May we all have an overflow of those things that our bodies can't hold all of it so we

232

need a hypothetical storage unit for the abundance. Not clothes. Not furniture. Not earthly possessions. But love. Peace. Happiness. And the ever hard to achieve - contentment.

Simplify. Start small, and get the excess stuff in your life completely away from you. You will find that contentedness and peace will overcome your feelings of stress, anxiety, and being in the rat race. We don't need a storage facility on every corner. We don't need that much junk to clutter our lives. Let's store up for ourselves treasures in Heaven where moth and rust do not destroy and where thieves will not break in and steal. Let us store up our fruits of the spirit and drown out all the excess earthly stuff that brings out the worst in all of us. Stay simple.

Training for Goofy

I signed up for the Walt Disney World Marathon in 2013. I was pretty readily convinced I should sign up for Goofy's Race and a Half Challenge. It is a half marathon on Saturday and a full marathon on Sunday. What was I thinking? I ran no less than 14 miles on a Saturday from June till December of that year. I missed a few runs but not many. I ran the majority of the runs barefooted with the five finger sleeves.

If you are running more than 3 miles at a time then it isn't for exercise. It is for some other reason. It may be to increase your mental stamina. It may be to purge demons from your head. It may be to socialize, or to get some time alone with your thoughts. Whatever the reason it isn't for exercise.

Three miles will be for exercise. The rest is a mission.

I would like to share a few of my favorite moments from my training season for Goofy.

My favorite running moment from the season was the 14.5 mile run where I got to know a friend much better. We talked about our children and she was listening to me ramble about this and that and suggested it was not right to keep these thoughts to myself. She suggested I become a motivational speaker and author. She had contacts that put me into the fast track and as you know, all this is reality now. This would not have happened had I not been training for Goofy. Many miles had been run over those 6 months and many of the worlds problems were solved while pounding the pavement.

235

One August Saturday, I had been up from attending my son's all night hockey tournament. I ran anyway. By mile 9 I was toast. One of my buddies grabbed my hand and said he was tired too and that we would share energy. It was super amazing to me how it really worked. We shared energy and both were able to finish the run. This moment would never have happened without training for Goofy.

We all discovered that peanut butter and jelly sandwiches are the best training fuel on the planet. They are even better than Gu or sport beans. One about mile 8 is perfect. Another at mile 16 is icing on the energy cake.

We finished an 18 mile run when one of my buddies suggested we sign up for the Loonies Midnight Marathon the next Saturday which is a marathon that starts at midnight. I said, "Wash your mouth out!" I was NOT running any midnight marathon. This beauty needs her rest.

I'm not gunna sugar coat the training for this event. It was hard. There were many times I wanted to give up and not train. It stinks to be out running for 4+ hours every Saturday. The people I trained with made it worth it. They are still some of my best friends.

On a 23 mile training run, at about mile 12, one of my buds asked me, "How are you doing?" I said, "I am NOT having fun." She didn't say anything but took off to catch up with some buds in front of us and yelled, "Hey Mr. Motivation! We have one back here not having fun!" He dropped back and gave me a pep talk I will never forget. I finished that run that day and had fun along the way thanks to my buddies.

December 23, 2013 was the next to the last training run for Goofy. December 27, we did 10 miles and December 28, we did 20 miles to prepare us for the back to back races at Disney. Our race was in January 2014. The training was about over and the fun would begin! I was so excited about this adventure.

I can't think of anyone I would rather go to Disney World and run farther than people should run than the Dopey crew. We were about to reach the culmination of lots of hard work and determination together in Orlando

Florida at the Happiest Place on Earth in January 2014!

Disney's Dopey Challenge

I ran one marathon, The Country Music Marathon Nashville in 2011, and swore I would never run another one. I hated it. It is too far, hideous training, and I am slow enough that it takes me too long to run one that I have to take my lunch along for the journey. My first marathon I packed Chick Fil A chicken nuggets and french fries. I ate them on Rosa Parks Boulevard.

Fast forward to 2013, January. My running goal for the year was to not run anything over 10 miles at a single time for the year. Until I started receiving email about the Disney Race in January. It was a race on my bucket list. I decided to sign up for the Marathon because I was a bit concerned that this item on my bucket list would not ever be checked off if I didn't proceed with it. A running buddy sent me another email asking me to run the Goofy Challenge. He felt like I could do it and he has a way of making you believe you can run to the moon. So I signed up. I became a part of the Dopey Crew even though I was only running the Goofy.

Training went well, was fun, made new friends, felt a sense of being a part of something spectacular, solved some world problems on the road, felt good about myself, proved some things, etc.

Thanksgiving Day I ran the Turkey Trot and with no explanation as to why or how, I hurt my hip. One minute I was fine and the next minute I was tossing my leg over my shoulder and hopping the last mile to the finish. I tried to heal it by resting it for two weeks and no improvement. I saw a sports medicine doctor who diagnosed me with a severe adductor strain. He said my injury would take me out of running for 6 weeks. The problem with this injury is that it gets no relief during the running process. It is used for every movement in running so it will only get worse if I try to use it. I followed his instructions to the letter of the law and did not run. I skipped the Rocket City Marathon that I had registered for. It killed me. Disney was more important. I missed several "crucial" training runs. My head was feeling like I was a loser and I would not be able to run Disney if I wasn't trained.

Arrival in Disney, the discovery is made that there is an extra Dopey bib amongst the group I was with. What is another 9.3 miles? So I took the bib and agreed to run the Dopey. I did not wear my Garmin for the 5K, 10K or half marathon. I enjoyed those races better than any races I have ever run. I felt so close to God as I watched the sun rise over the World Showcase at Epcot in the 5K.

Since we had to get up at 2am Nashville time every morning to start each race, of course it was dark when we ran. In each race, I got to watch the sun rise over some part of Disney. I was humbled to watch it go from dark to light over so many magical places in the compound. Gorgeous work, Lord!

In the 10K, I enjoyed the time I ran next to a lady who was pushing her leg in a cart because she was injured. We talked about how injury stinks and she wept as we talked stating that she just felt blessed to be there moving forward. I felt blessed from my time running with her.

In the half marathon, my best running buddy and I enjoyed ourselves thoroughly. We stopped and had our pictures made with every character and laughed in between. We had the worst clock time we have had in that race that day. But we had the best time we have ever had in a race. We smelled a lot of roses and solved a lot of problems.

On Thursday, 5K day, My buddy and I bought a park hopper pass and went to 3 Disney parks. We agreed that a Mickey

Mouse ice cream treat qualified as carb loading!

We had the best time ever. Some of our group were concerned that we would suffer come Sunday when it is marathon day since we spent the day going to parks. It was a truly magical day. We laughed until our sides hurt. We had the goal of riding all the roller coasters in the park. We were successful for the most part. We learned to read a map and discovered that just because you can see the ride doesn't mean you are heading toward it. We filled our personal fuel tanks full to overflowing by visiting the parks that day. They are memories I will never forget.

When we got back to the condo, I threw a load of clothes in the washer. When one comes to run two races and ends up running 4 races, one needs to wash their running clothes. I accidentally washed my race bib. In Disney, you have to wear your same bib for two races. So Dopey's had two bibs, one for the 5K and 10K and one for the half and full. My bib was pretty mangled after a bath. You could barely read my corral number and the wording on the bib. I looked like Job's Turkey wearing my washed bib. But I decided I liked washed bibs. It made me unique.

The marathon had its own set of challenges just because of the excess of mileage. I had a firm plan for success. I would run 3/1 splits, not pay attention to mileage or pace, but simply focus on running for 3 minutes. I can do that. I had already taken a lot of pictures so decided that there was no character that would make me want to stop any more. I would start the marathon and do my splits and not stop until I got to the finish line. I would pay no attention to miles or how far I still had to go. I did not imagine that a roller coaster would be open. At mile 12.5, I noticed while running through Animal Kingdom that Expedition Everest was open.

It was the one roller coaster that my friend and I did not get to ride when we went to the parks. When I got to the entrance to Everest, I asked the cast member if I could ride. They said, "Of Course! Hop in the fast pass lane!"

It was a no brainer for me. I HAD to ride. I ran all the way up the cue line so as not to lose any more time on my marathon. I rode the ride and had the most EPIC ride ever!

It was groovy to be able to distract myself with a little roller coaster reward for running hard for the first half. After the roller coaster ride, I ate my lunch that I had packed. For this marathon I packed a peanut butter and jelly sandwich and chips. It was yummy and fueled my for the second half of my race. I finished strong in my marathon, Did not stop again until I saw the finish line. It was the most epic marathon experience ever. I got a personal record in the marathon by 11 minutes even with the extra time it took to ride the roller coaster at the half way mark. I would not trade my experience for anything. It was the best day of my life.

The marathon was the best as far as scenery. You got to run through all 4 parks as well as on the Disney track for the Richard Petty Experience, and through the ESPN Wide World of Sports where the Braves have their spring training. We got to run on the Braves field(around the perimeter of the

247

grass). It was incredibly entertaining scenery, very flat course, and fun around every corner.

After the race, I shopped at the Disney Running Merchandise booth at the finish line and then returned to the car. My other running friends, of course, were already there and were laid out from tiredness of running. I bounced up and said, "I have been shopping and I rode a roller coaster in the middle of the marathon and still got a PR!" A PR is a personal record. They all just looked at me. I thought they all would have ridden the ride but they didn't even see it.

I rapidly realized that I ran a different race. I OWNED my marathon. I made it all mine. Riding a roller coaster in the middle of a marathon is totally me. Since I washed my bib, the writing was faded badly and my bib said the Nopey Challenge rather than the Dopey Challenge. Thus, the ride was open and no one else saw it, and the OWNING of my marathon. Jennifer Anglin-Queen of the Nopey Challenge!

I will be washing my bibs from now on.

You are Enough

It is my prayer that my stories included in this book have helped you notice that you are enough. You are enough in your own life, in the lives of those that you love, and the lives of those you meet. Not everyone will like you, and that is ok. Even if some don't like you, you are still enough. You do not need to prove your worth to anyone. Your worth is in

Jesus Christ and Him crucified. With your flaws, you are enough. With your shortcomings, you are enough. With your triumphs, you are enough. With your tragedies, you are enough. In a world of too much, you are enough.

Stay tuned to my website, www.funthoughtsonlife.com where the sequel to Fun Thoughts on Life will be released in late 2019. The title is Muddy Sunflowers Still Face the Light by Jennifer Anglin.

On my website, you can contact me for one on one life coaching, motivational speaking, and to purchase my books and merchandise.

www.funthoughtsonlife.com